FAVORITE BRAND NAME™

Best-Loved Food of the '50s

Publications International, Ltd.

Favorite Brand Name Recipes at www.fbnr.com

Pictured on the front cover: Southern Buttermilk Fried Chicken *(page 64).*

Pictured on jacket flaps *(front to back):* The Famous Lipton® California Dip *(page 22)* and Country Sausage Macaroni and Cheese *(page 104).*

Pictured on the back cover *(left to right):* Steak Hash *(page 38),* Hungarian Goulash Casserole *(page 110)* and Peach Tapioca *(page 242).*

ISBN-13: 978-1-4127-2554-5
ISBN-10: 1-4127-2554-2

Library of Congress Control Number: 2006935727

Manufactured in China.

8 7 6 5 4 3 2 1

Microwave Cooking: Microwave ovens vary in wattage. Use the cooking times as guidelines and check for doneness before adding more time.

Preparation/Cooking Times: Preparation times are based on the approximate amount of time required to assemble the recipe before cooking, baking, chilling or serving. These times include preparation steps such as measuring, chopping and mixing. The fact that some preparations and cooking can be done simultaneously is taken into account. Preparation of optional ingredients and serving suggestions is not included.

Table of Contents

Introduction 4

Cocktail Nibbles 8

Boss Beef and Pork 32

Boppin' Birds 60

Cruisin' Casseroles 88

Luscious Luau 114

Patio Daddy-O 138

Cool Cat Cakes 166

Kookie Cookies 194

Dainty Desserts 222

Acknowledgments 249

Index 250

American Food in the Fifties

Postwar America was a rich country. There were more jobs, more homes being built, more money, and of course, more babies. Men home from the war were now driving off to work in their shiny cars with fins. Suburbia promised freedom, space and a gracious life. Women were happy (or supposed to be) in ultra-clean kitchens equipped with every modern appliance. Mom could buy an array of canned goods and frozen foods that would make cooking gourmet dinners as easy as wielding a can opener. The truth was that many convenience products, such as luncheon meat and powdered milk, actually began as wartime technologies invented to feed the troops. Now they were repackaged and advertised as the clever way to end kitchen drudgery.

Casseroles are Queen

Canned cream soups had been around since 1914, but during the 1950s they became the sauce of American cuisine. Combining them with a protein and some canned or frozen vegetables was the modern way to get dinner on the table and leave the savvy homemaker time to attend the PTA meeting or take the kids to the park. From tuna noodle casserole to tamale pie, many of these one-dish wonders are still favorites.

A Fifties Luau Menu

Wild Hawaiian
Cocktail Meatballs
(page 17)

Ambrosia
(page 122)

South Seas Shrimp
and Mango
(page 126)

Hawaiian Ribs
(page 130)

Tropical Pork Chops
(page 129)

Tidal Wave Cocoa
Almond Mousse
(page 128)

Barbecues Boom

Well-manicured lawns and big backyards were the perfect place for a barbecue. Cooking over a fire with all its caveman connotations was considered man's work. Now that large tender cuts of beef and pork were available and affordable, charcoal-grilled steak was a necessary luxury—and what could be more masculine than slapping a hunk of raw meat onto a searing hot grill. (Of course, the lady of the house was still expected to buy the food, plan the party, play hostess and clean up.)

The Perfect Dip with the Perfect Martini

No fifties cocktail party was complete without a buffet that included a cheese ball and at least one dip. Entertaining was serious business and so were martinis. While the drink had been around since before the turn of the century, making the perfect dry martini became the source of endless discussion and raucous experimentation.

Exotic Becomes Mainstream

Pupu platters and mai tais served amid frowning tiki gods made restaurants like Trader Vic's a huge success. At home Polynesian-themed parties, complete with umbrellas in the drinks, were considered very up-to-date. The yen for the exotic extended to tropical fruit. Pineapple and coconut ended up in some unusual, but distinctly American, concoctions. (How about hot dogs baked in pineapple sweet and sour sauce?)

Intro

The Can-Opener Gourmet

Americans were traveling to Europe in record numbers and yearned for gourmet, continental dishes at home. Of course, the sophisticated way to achieve classic cuisine was with convenience foods. For beef stroganoff or lobster thermidor, cream of mushroom soup was the starting place. For a fancy "en croûte" entrée, almost any food could be (and was) wrapped in packaged pie crust.

Dining Tables Turn into TV Trays

Television sets were becoming more affordable and there were more programs to watch. In 1952 the first frozen dinners appeared, but it wasn't until three years later that the idea caught on with a package designed to look like a TV screen. For a mere 98 cents, there was turkey, stuffing, gravy, whipped sweet potatoes and peas all snuggled into separate compartments in an aluminum tray.

A Fifties Gourmet Dinner Party Menu

Tuna Mushroom Pâté with Orange Liqueur
(page 28)

Venetian Canapés
(page 30)

Beef Wellington
(page 50)

Potatoes with Parsley Butter

Tossed Bibb Lettuce in Blue Cheese Dressing

Crêpes Suzettes
(page 230)

Intro

A Fifties Cocktail Party Menu

Dry Martinis
(Clam & Tomato Cocktails
for non-drinkers)

Molded Crab Mousse
(page 10)

Spicy Spam™ Party Dip
(page 16)

Zesty Liver Pâté
(page 26)

Coffee

Chocolate Petits Fours
(page 234)

The Fifties Legacy

The food of the fifties is more than a historical curiosity. It offers lessons and recipes we can still learn from. The decade ushered in the beginning of the wonders of convenience foods. It was also the start of a new freedom—an opening of boundaries and dropping of barriers. Now American cooking encompassed not only pot roast and tuna noodle casserole, but chicken cacciatore and coq au vin. Home cooks learned not just from their mothers, but from travel, books and television cooks like Julia Child. Women went to work in record numbers and still came home to make the dinner. Here in the 21st century, just as in the fifties, preparing food with loving hands for family and friends may be a necessary chore, but it is also a creative outlet and a labor of love.

Cocktail Nibbles

The modern '50s hostess prided herself on creating a wonderful array of hors d'oeuvres with the help of brand new labor-saving products, such as canned meat and onion soup mix. Gracious entertaining was a welcome excuse to impress guests with a chafing dish of saucy meatballs or a buffet table filled with trendy dips and canapés. Try out some of these favorites at your next party and make cocktail history all over again.

Spicy SPAM™ Party Dip (page 16)

Molded Crab Mousse

    2 cans (6 ounces each) crabmeat *or* 2 cups fresh shelled crabmeat
    1 cup (4 ounces) shredded Colby cheese
    $^1/_2$ cup finely chopped celery
    $^1/_4$ cup finely chopped onion
    $^1/_4$ cup finely chopped red bell pepper
    $^1/_4$ cup finely chopped green bell pepper
    1 cup sour cream
    $^1/_2$ cup mayonnaise
    $^1/_4$ cup chili sauce
    2 tablespoons lemon juice
    3 tablespoons cold water
    1 tablespoon unflavored gelatin
       Cucumber slices (optional)
       Fresh dill sprigs (optional)

1. Lightly spray 1-quart fish-shaped mold with nonstick cooking spray.

2. Place crabmeat in large bowl. Pick out and discard any shell pieces or cartilage. Add cheese, celery, onion and bell peppers; toss gently.

3. Combine sour cream, mayonnaise, chili sauce and lemon juice in small bowl. Pour cold water into small saucepan; stir in gelatin. Cook over low heat, stirring constantly, until thoroughly dissolved. Stir quickly into sour cream mixture.

4. Fold sour cream mixture into crab mixture; spoon into prepared mold. Cover with plastic wrap; refrigerate 3 hours or until set. Unmold onto serving platter. Garnish with cucumber slices and dill sprigs.   *Makes 32 servings*

Molded Crab Mousse

Cocktail Nibbles

Crab and Artichoke Stuffed Mushrooms

$^1/_2$ **pound Florida blue crab meat**

1 **(14-ounce) can artichoke hearts, drained and finely chopped**

1 **cup mayonnaise***

$^1/_2$ **cup grated Parmesan cheese**

$^1/_4$ **teaspoon lemon pepper seasoning**

$^1/_8$ **teaspoon salt**

$^1/_8$ **teaspoon cayenne pepper**

30 **large fresh Florida mushrooms**

Or, you can substitute mixture of $^1/_2$ cup mayonnaise and $^1/_2$ cup plain yogurt.

Remove any pieces of shell or cartilage from crabmeat. Combine crabmeat, artichoke hearts, mayonnaise, Parmesan cheese and seasonings; mix until well blended. Remove stems from mushrooms and fill the caps with crabmeat mixture. Place in a lightly greased, shallow baking dish. Bake in a preheated 400°F oven for 10 minutes or until hot and bubbly.   *Makes 30 appetizer servings*

Favorite recipe from **Florida Department of Agriculture and Consumer Services, Bureau of Seafood and Aquaculture**

Cocktail Nibbles

Brandy-Soaked Scallops

- 1 pound bacon, cut in half crosswise
- 2 pounds small sea scallops
- 1/2 cup brandy
- 1/3 cup olive oil
- 2 tablespoons chopped fresh parsley
- 1 clove garlic, minced
- 1 teaspoon black pepper
- 1/2 teaspoon salt
- 1/2 teaspoon onion powder

1. Wrap one piece bacon around each scallop; secure with toothpick, if necessary. Place wrapped scallops in 13×9-inch baking dish.

2. Combine brandy, oil, parsley, garlic, pepper, salt and onion powder in small bowl; mix well. Pour mixture over scallops; cover and marinate in refrigerator at least 4 hours.

3. Preheat broiler. Remove scallops from marinade; discard marinade. Arrange scallops on rack of broiler pan. Broil 4 inches from heat 7 to 10 minutes or until bacon is browned. Turn and broil 5 minutes more or until scallops are opaque; remove toothpicks. *Makes 8 servings*

helpful hint:

There are two types of scallops available: sea scallops and bay scallops. Sea scallops are more widely available but they're less tender. Bay scallops are smaller, slightly sweeter and more expensive. Both varieties can also be found frozen.

Brandy-Soaked Scallops

Cocktail Nibbles

Spicy SPAM™ Party Dip

- 2 (8-ounce) packages cream cheese, softened
- 1 (12-ounce) can SPAM® Classic, grated
- 2 tablespoons Worcestershire sauce
- 1 teaspoon CHI-CHI'S® Salsa
  Dash cayenne pepper
- 1 cup finely chopped green or red bell pepper
- ½ cup chopped celery
- ¼ cup chopped onion
- 2 tablespoons chopped fresh cilantro
  Crackers, chips and/or vegetables

In medium bowl, combine cream cheese, SPAM®, Worcestershire sauce, salsa and cayenne pepper. Beat at medium speed of electric mixer until smooth. Stir in bell pepper, celery, onion and cilantro. Cover and refrigerate 1 hour. Serve with crackers, chips and vegetables. *Makes 4 cups dip*

Oysters Romano

- 12 oysters, shucked and on the half-shell
- 2 slices bacon, cut into 12 (1-inch) pieces
- ½ cup Italian-seasoned dry bread crumbs
- 2 tablespoons butter, melted
- ½ teaspoon garlic salt
- 6 tablespoons grated Romano or Parmesan
  Fresh chives (optional)

1. Preheat oven to 375°F. Place shells with oysters on baking sheet. Top each oyster with 1 piece bacon. Bake 10 minutes or until bacon is crisp.

2. Meanwhile, combine bread crumbs, butter and garlic salt in small bowl. Spoon mixture over oysters; top with cheese. Bake 5 to 10 minutes or until cheese melts. Garnish with chives. *Makes 4 appetizer servings*

Wild Hawaiian Cocktail Meatballs

1 can (15 1/4 ounces) pineapple chunks in juice, undrained
14 ounces ground chicken
1 cup cooked wild rice
1/4 cup finely chopped green bell pepper
1/4 cup fine cracker crumbs
1 egg
1 teaspoon onion salt
1/4 teaspoon ground ginger
1 tablespoon vegetable oil
1 cup sweet and sour sauce

Drain pineapple, reserving juice. In large bowl, combine chicken, wild rice, bell pepper, cracker crumbs, 2 tablespoons pineapple juice, egg, onion salt and ginger; mix well. Form mixture into 1-inch meatballs. In large skillet, heat oil over medium heat. Brown meatballs; drain. Add reserved pineapple and remaining juice; cover and cook over medium heat 10 to 15 minutes or until meatballs are no longer pink in center. Stir sweet and sour sauce into meatballs and pineapple; cook 4 to 5 minutes or until mixture is heated through. Serve with frilled toothpicks.

Makes 35 to 40 appetizers

Note: For main dish, serve meatballs over cooked rice or noodles. Makes 5 main-dish servings.

Favorite recipe from **Minnesota Cultivated Wild Rice Council**

Blue Crab Stuffed Tomatoes

$^1/_2$ pound Florida blue crab meat

10 plum tomatoes

$^1/_2$ cup finely chopped celery

$^1/_3$ cup plain low fat yogurt

2 tablespoons minced green onion

2 tablespoons finely chopped red bell pepper

$^1/_2$ teaspoon lemon juice

$^1/_4$ teaspoon salt

$^1/_8$ teaspoon black pepper

Remove any shell or cartilage from crabmeat.

Cut tomatoes in half lengthwise. Carefully scoop out centers of tomatoes; discard pulp. Invert on paper towels.

Combine crabmeat, celery, yogurt, onion, red pepper, lemon juice, salt and black pepper. Mix well.

Fill tomato halves with crab mixture. Refrigerate 2 hours.   *Makes 20 appetizers*

Favorite recipe from **Florida Department of Agriculture and Consumer Services, Bureau of Seafood and Aquaculture**

Blue Crab Stuffed Tomatoes

Pecan Cheese Ball

   1 package (8 ounces) cream cheese, softened
   $\frac{1}{4}$ cup finely chopped fresh parsley
   2 tablespoons finely chopped fresh chives
   $\frac{1}{2}$ teaspoon Worcestershire sauce
     Dash hot pepper sauce
   $\frac{3}{4}$ cup finely chopped pecans
     Assorted crackers

1. Combine all ingredients except pecans and crackers in medium bowl. Cover; refrigerate until firm. Form cheese mixture into ball. Roll in pecans.

2. Store tightly wrapped in plastic wrap in refrigerator. Allow cheese ball to soften at room temperature before serving with crackers.   *Makes 1 cheese ball*

Variation: Form cheese mixture into 12 (1 $\frac{1}{2}$-inch) balls. Roll in paprika, chopped herbs (such as parsley, watercress or basil) or chopped green olives, instead of pecans.

Tip: For a hostess gift, give a Pecan Cheese Ball with an assortment of other cheeses, a wooden cheese board and jar of imported pickles or mustard.

Top to bottom: Pecan Cheese Balls (variations) and Cheddar Cheese Spread (Page 27)

Cocktail Nibbles

The Famous Lipton® California Dip

1 envelope LIPTON® RECIPE SECRETS® Onion Soup Mix
1 container (16 ounces) regular or light sour cream

1. In medium bowl, blend all ingredients; chill at least 2 hours.

2. Serve with your favorite dippers.   *Makes about 2 cups dip*

Tip: For a creamier dip, add more sour cream.

Sensational Spinach Dip: Add 1 package (10 ounces) frozen chopped spinach, thawed and squeezed dry.

California Seafood Dip: Add 1 cup finely chopped cooked clams, crabmeat or shrimp, 1/4 cup chili sauce and 1 tablespoon horseradish.

California Bacon Dip: Add 1/3 cup crumbled cooked bacon or bacon bits.

California Blue Cheese Dip: Add 1/4 pound crumbled blue cheese and 1/4 cup finely chopped walnuts.

The Famous Lipton® California Dip

Cocktail Nibbles

Shrimp Toast

1 2 large shrimp, shelled and deveined, tails intact
1 egg
2 tablespoons plus 1 ½ teaspoons cornstarch
¼ teaspoon salt
   Dash black pepper
3 slices white sandwich bread, crusts removed, quartered
1 hard-cooked egg yolk, cut into ½-inch pieces
1 slice (1 ounce) cooked ham, cut into ½-inch pieces
1 green onion, finely chopped
   Vegetable oil for frying

1. Cut deep slit down back of each shrimp; press gently with fingers to flatten.

2. Beat egg, cornstarch, salt and pepper in large bowl until blended. Add shrimp; toss to coat well.

3. Drain each shrimp and press, cut side down, into each piece of bread. Brush or rub small amount of remaining egg mixture onto each shrimp.

4. Place one piece each of egg yolk and ham and scant ¼ teaspoon green onion on top of each shrimp.

5. Heat oil in wok or large skillet over medium-high heat to 375°F. Add three or four bread pieces at a time; cook 1 to 2 minutes on each side or until golden. Drain on paper towels. Garnish, if desired. *Makes 1 dozen toasts*

Tip: To keep the shrimp from flattening during cooking, spoon hot oil over the shrimp toasts until cooked through instead of turning them over.

Shrimp Toasts

Cocktail Nibbles

Zesty Liver Pâté

1/3 cup butter or margarine
1 pound chicken livers
3/4 cup coarsely chopped green onions
3/4 cup chopped fresh parsley
1/2 cup dry white wine
3/4 teaspoon **TABASCO**® brand Pepper Sauce
1/2 teaspoon salt
Crackers or French bread

Melt butter in large saucepan; add chicken livers, onions and parsley. Sauté until livers are evenly browned and cooked through. Transfer to blender or food processor container. Add wine, TABASCO® Sauce and salt; cover. Process until smooth. Pour into decorative crock-style jar with lid. Chill until thick enough to spread. Serve with crackers or French bread.   *Makes about 2 cups pâté*

Smoked Salmon Appetizers

1/4 cup cream cheese, softened
1 tablespoon chopped fresh dill *or* 1 teaspoon dried dill weed
1/8 teaspoon ground red pepper
4 ounces thinly sliced smoked salmon or lox
24 melba toast rounds
Fresh dill sprigs (optional)

1. Combine cream cheese, dill and red pepper in small bowl; stir to blend. Spread evenly over each slice of salmon. Roll up salmon slices jelly-roll style. Place on plate; cover with plastic wrap. Chill at least 1 hour or up to 4 hours before serving.

2. Using sharp knife, cut salmon rolls crosswise into 3/4-inch pieces. Place pieces, cut side down, on melba rounds. Garnish each salmon roll with dill sprig. Serve cold or at room temperature.   *Makes about 2 dozen appetizers*

Cheddar Cheese Spread

3 ounces white Cheddar cheese, cubed

3 ounces yellow Cheddar cheese, cubed

1 package (3 ounces) cream cheese, cubed

6 green onions, white parts only, finely chopped

2 tablespoons butter or margarine, softened

2 tablespoons dry sherry

1 teaspoon Dijon mustard

1 teaspoon Worcestershire sauce

$^1/_4$ teaspoon salt (optional)

Dash hot pepper sauce (optional)

2 tablespoons finely chopped chives

Assorted crackers

1. Place all ingredients except chives and crackers in food processor or blender; process until smooth. Add chives; pulse to mix in.

2. Transfer to serving bowl. Cover; refrigerate. Allow spread to soften at room temperature before serving. Serve with crackers.   *Makes about 2 cups spread*

Tip: To give Cheddar Cheese Spread as a hostess gift, place cheese mixture in a crock or gift container before refrigerating. Include a box of crackers.

Tuna Mushroom Pâté with Orange Liqueur

- 2 cloves garlic
- 1/2 medium white onion
- 2 tablespoons butter
- 1 jar (4 1/2 ounces) sliced mushrooms, drained
- 2 tablespoons orange liqueur or orange juice
- 1 package (8 ounces) cream cheese, softened
- 1 (7-ounce) STARKIST Flavor Fresh Pouch® Tuna (Albacore or Chunk Light)
- 2 tablespoons fresh parsley leaves
- 1 teaspoon grated orange peel
- 1/4 teaspoon salt
- 1/4 teaspoon coarsely ground black pepper
- 1/2 cup toasted slivered almonds (optional)
  Crackers or raw vegetables

In food processor bowl with metal blade, drop garlic through feed tube while processing. Add onion; pulse on and off to chop coarsely. In small skillet, melt butter over medium heat. Add garlic and onion; sauté until onion is soft. Add mushrooms and liqueur; cook until liquid evaporates. Cool.

In same food processor bowl with metal blade, place cream cheese, tuna, parsley, orange peel, salt and pepper. Pulse on and off to blend. Add cooled onion-mushroom mixture; pulse on and off to blend. Stir in almonds, if desired. Spoon into 1-quart serving bowl; chill several hours or overnight. Serve with crackers.

Makes about 12 servings

Prep Time: 20 minutes

Tuna Mushroom Pâté with Orange Liqueur

29

Venetian Canapés

  1 2 slices firm white bread
  5 tablespoons butter, divided
  2 tablespoons all-purpose flour
$^1/_2$ cup milk
  3 ounces fresh mushrooms (about 9 medium), finely chopped
  6 tablespoons grated Parmesan cheese, divided
  2 teaspoons anchovy paste
$^1/_4$ teaspoon salt
$^1/_8$ teaspoon black pepper
     Green and black olive slices, red and green bell pepper strips and rolled anchovy
        fillets (optional)

1. Preheat oven to 350°F. Cut 2 rounds from each bread slice with 2-inch round cutter. Melt 3 tablespoons butter in small saucepan. Brush both sides of bread rounds lightly with butter. Bake bread rounds on ungreased baking sheet 5 to 6 minutes per side or until golden. Remove to wire rack. Cool completely. *Increase oven temperature to 425°F.*

2. Melt remaining 2 tablespoons butter in same saucepan. Stir in flour; cook and stir over medium heat until bubbly. Whisk in milk; cook and stir 1 minute or until sauce thickens and bubbles. (Sauce will be very thick.) Place mushrooms in large bowl; stir in sauce, 3 tablespoons cheese, anchovy paste, salt and black pepper until well blended.

3. Spread 1 heaping teaspoonful mushroom mixture onto each toast round; place on ungreased baking sheets. Sprinkle remaining 3 tablespoons cheese over bread rounds. Bake 5 to 7 minutes or until tops are light brown. Garnish with olive slices, bell pepper strips, and anchovy fillets. Serve warm.   *Makes 24 canapés*

Venetian Canapés

Boss Beef and Pork

After suffering through the lean pantries of the war years, Americans celebrated the new abundance with meals based around big hunks of meat. Roasts, steaks and chops graced even middle-class tables. SPAM™ and other canned meats that had been developed for the military were popular during peacetime, too. Now classic '50s entrées, from fancy Beef Wellington to down-home Steak Hash, are yours to enjoy again.

Sirloin Steak Monte Carlo (page 41)

Double Cheese Veal Cutlets

- **2** tablespoons butter
- **1** pound veal cutlets
  Salt and black pepper
- **4** cups **CLAMATO®** Tomato Cocktail
  Pinch of dried thyme
- **2** tablespoons grated Parmesan cheese
- **1** cup **(4 ounces)** shredded Swiss cheese
- **1** avocado, peeled and sliced

1. In large skillet, melt butter. Brown cutlets a few at a time, 2 minutes on each side. Remove and sprinkle lightly with salt and pepper.

2. Return veal to skillet, overlapping cutlets. Add Clamato and thyme; simmer 5 to 10 minutes, or until veal is tender. Arrange veal in ovenproof serving dish and pour sauce over veal. Sprinkle with Parmesan cheese and Swiss cheese. Place under preheated broiler 5 minutes, or until cheese is melted. Top cutlets with avocado slices. *Makes 6 to 8 servings*

helpful hint:

To slice an avocado, press the center of the knife blade into the fruit, making an even cut all the way around. Then twist the two halves of the avocado apart. Scoop out the pit with a spoon. You can then slice the avocado right inside the peel.

Double Cheese Veal Cutlets

Pork Schnitzel

4 boneless pork chops, cut $1/4$ inch thick
$1/2$ cup cornflake or cracker crumbs
1 egg, lightly beaten
Black pepper
2 to 4 teaspoons olive oil, divided
$1/3$ cup lemon juice
$1/4$ cup chicken broth

1. Preheat oven to 200°F. Place ovenproof platter or baking sheet in oven. Trim fat from pork chops. Place pork chops between layers of waxed paper; pound with smooth side of mallet to $1/8$-inch thickness.

2. Place crumbs in medium bowl. Dip 1 pork chop at a time in egg; gently shake off excess. Dip in crumbs to coat both sides. Place breaded pork chops in single layer on plate. Sprinkle with pepper.

3. Heat 2 teaspoons oil in large skillet over medium-high heat until hot. Add pork chops in single layer in batches if necessary. Cook 1 minute or until golden brown. Turn; cook 1 minute or until golden brown and pork is no longer pink in center. Transfer to platter in oven to keep warm. Repeat with any remaining pork chops, adding oil as needed to prevent meat from sticking to skillet.

4. Remove skillet from heat. Add lemon juice and broth. Stir to scrape cooked bits from bottom of pan. Return to heat; bring to a boil, stirring constantly, until liquid is reduced to 3 to 4 tablespoons.

5. Remove platter from oven. Pour lemon sauce over meat. *Makes 4 servings*

Prep and Cook Time: 20 minutes

Pork Schnitzel

37

Boss Beef and Pork

Steak Hash

 2 tablespoons vegetable oil
 1 green bell pepper, chopped
 $^1/_2$ medium onion, chopped
 1 pound russet potatoes, baked and chopped
 $^1/_2$ pound cooked steak or roast beef, cut into 1-inch cubes
     Salt and black pepper
 $^1/_4$ cup (1 ounce) shredded Monterey Jack cheese
 4 eggs

1. Heat oil in medium skillet over medium heat. Add bell pepper and onion; cook until tender. Stir in potatoes; reduce heat to low. Cover and cook, stirring occasionally, about 10 minutes or until potatoes are hot.

2. Stir in steak; season with salt and pepper. Sprinkle with cheese. Cover; cook 5 minutes or until steak is hot and cheese is melted. Meanwhile, prepare eggs as desired; top each serving with 1 egg. *Makes 4 servings*

Down-Home Pork and Beans

     Nonstick cooking spray
 $^3/_4$ cup *each* sliced onion and diced green bell pepper
 2 cloves garlic, minced
 1 can (15 ounces) white beans, rinsed and drained
 1 can (10$^3/_4$ ounces) condensed tomato soup, undiluted
 10 ounces pork tenderloin, trimmed and cubed
 $^1/_2$ cup packed brown sugar
 $^1/_4$ cup barbecue sauce
 $^1/_2$ teaspoon salt

Spray large saucepan with cooking spray. Add onion, bell pepper and garlic; cook and stir until tender. Add beans, soup, pork, brown sugar, barbecue sauce and salt. Cover; simmer 1 hour. *Makes 6 servings*

Steak Hash

39

Roast Pork Chops with Apple and Cabbage

- 3 teaspoons olive oil, divided
- 1/2 medium onion, thinly sliced
- 1 teaspoon dried thyme
- 2 cloves garlic, minced
- 4 pork chops (6 to 8 ounces each), 1 inch thick
  Salt and black pepper
- 1/4 cup cider vinegar
- 1 tablespoon packed brown sugar
- 1 large McIntosh apple, chopped
- 1/2 (8-ounce) package shredded coleslaw mix

1. Preheat over to 375°F.

2. Heat 2 teaspoons oil in large ovenproof skillet over medium-high heat. Add onion; cook, covered, 4 to 6 minutes or until tender, stirring often. Add thyme and garlic; cook and stir 30 seconds. Transfer to small bowl; set aside.

3. Add remaining 1 teaspoon oil to same skillet. Season pork chops with salt and pepper. Place in skillet; cook 2 minutes on each side or until browned. Remove pork chops from skillet; set aside.

4. Remove skillet from heat. Add vinegar, brown sugar and pepper; stir to dissolve sugar and scrape cooked bits from skillet. Add onion mixture, apple and coleslaw mix; do not stir.

5. Arrange pork chops on top of cabbage mixture, overlapping if necessary. Cover pan; place in oven. Bake 15 minutes or until pork chops are just barely pink in center.

Makes 4 servings

Sirloin Steak Monte Carlo

2 tablespoons olive or vegetable oil
1 3/4 pounds sirloin steak
1/2 cup sliced onion
1 large clove garlic, minced
1/4 cup pine nuts
1 can (**14.5** ounces) **CONTADINA**® Italian-Style Stewed Tomatoes, undrained
2 tablespoons capers
1/2 teaspoon dried oregano leaves, crushed
1/2 teaspoon dried basil leaves, crushed
1/4 teaspoon crushed red pepper flakes

1. Heat oil in large skillet over medium-high heat. Add steak; cook 4 to 5 minutes on each side for medium-rare.

2. Remove steak to platter, reserving any drippings in skillet; cover steak with foil to keep warm.

3. Add onion, garlic and pine nuts to skillet; sauté 5 minutes or until onion is tender and nuts are lightly toasted.

4. Add undrained tomatoes, capers, oregano, basil and red pepper flakes; simmer, uncovered, 5 minutes. Serve over steak. *Makes 4 to 6 servings*

French Bistro Ham

2 pounds sliced HILLSHIRE FARM® Ham

DIJON GLAZE
¼ cup juices from cooked **HILLSHIRE FARM®** Ham
2 tablespoons Dijon mustard
2 tablespoons butter or margarine

PARSLEY POTATOES
1 pound small new potatoes
3 tablespoons butter
¼ cup chopped parsley
1 teaspoon salt
¼ teaspoon black pepper

SAUERKRAUT
1 pound sauerkraut
8 juniper berries, crushed (optional)

Prepare Ham according to directions on package. Reserve juices from cooked ham; set aside for Dijon Glaze.

For Dijon Glaze, mix reserved cooking juices and mustard in small bowl. Stir in butter and allow to melt.

For Parsley Potatoes, bring 4 quarts water to a boil in large saucepan over high heat. Boil potatoes until tender, about 20 minutes; drain. Melt butter in large skillet; add potatoes, parsley, salt and pepper, shaking skillet to coat potatoes.

For Sauerkraut, drain sauerkraut of most of its juices. Place in small saucepan with juniper berries, if desired. Heat gently over low heat about 7 minutes or until warmed through.

Serve Dijon Glaze over ham. Serve Parsley Potatoes and Sauerkraut alongside ham.

Makes 6 servings

French Bistro Ham

Hungarian Beef Goulash

$1/4$ cup all-purpose flour
1 tablespoon Hungarian sweet paprika
$1 1/2$ teaspoons salt
$1/2$ teaspoon Hungarian hot paprika
$1/2$ teaspoon black pepper
2 pounds beef stew meat
$1/4$ cup vegetable oil, divided
1 large onion, chopped
4 cloves garlic, minced
2 cans (about 14 ounces each) beef broth
1 can ($14 1/2$ ounces) stewed tomatoes, undrained
1 cup water
1 tablespoon dried marjoram
1 large green bell pepper, chopped
3 cups uncooked thin egg noodles
Sour cream

1. Combine flour, sweet paprika, salt, hot paprika and black pepper in large resealable food storage bag. Add half of beef. Seal bag; shake to coat well. Remove beef; set aside. Repeat with remaining beef.

2. Heat $4 1/2$ teaspoons oil in Dutch oven over medium heat until hot. Add half of beef; brown on all sides. Transfer to large bowl. Repeat with $4 1/2$ teaspoons oil and remaining beef; transfer to same bowl.

3. Heat remaining 1 tablespoon oil in same Dutch oven. Add onion and garlic; cook 8 minutes or until tender, stirring often.

4. Return beef and any accumulated juices to Dutch oven. Add broth, tomatoes with juice, water and marjoram. Bring to a boil over medium-high heat. Reduce heat to medium-low; cover and simmer $1 1/2$ hours or until meat is tender, stirring once.

5. Stir in bell pepper and noodles; cover. Simmer about 8 minutes or until noodles are tender, stirring once. Ladle into soup bowls; top with sour cream.

Makes 8 servings

Hungarian Beef Goulash

Filet Mignon with Tarragon Butter

2 (8-ounce) trimmed beef tenderloin steaks (1 1/4 to 1 1/2 inches thick)
2 teaspoons olive oil
1/4 teaspoon kosher salt
1/8 teaspoon freshly ground black pepper
2 tablespoons unsalted butter
1 clove garlic, minced
2 teaspoons chopped fresh tarragon *or* 3/4 teaspoon dried tarragon

1. Rub steaks with olive oil. Season with salt and pepper; and let stand at room temperature 15 minutes.

2. Heat medium skillet over medium-high heat. Cook steaks about 10 minutes, turning once, to 140°F for rare or to desired doneness. Transfer to serving plate and tent loosely with foil.

3. Melt butter in same skillet until it begins to brown slightly, scraping up any browned bits. Add garlic; cook until fragrant, about 15 seconds. Stir in tarragon. Pour sauce over steaks; serve immediately. *Makes 2 servings*

Filet Mignon with Tarragon Butter

47

Swedish Meatballs

1 1/2 cups fresh bread crumbs
1 cup (1/2 pint) heavy cream
2 tablespoons butter, divided
1 small onion, chopped
1 pound ground beef
1/2 pound ground pork
3 tablespoons chopped fresh parsley, divided
1 1/2 teaspoons salt
1/4 teaspoon ground allspice
1/4 teaspoon black pepper
1 cup beef broth
1 cup sour cream
1 tablespoon all-purpose flour

1. Combine bread crumbs and cream in small bowl; mix well. Let stand 10 minutes.

2. Melt 1 tablespoon butter in large skillet over medium heat. Add onion; cook and stir 5 minutes or until onion is tender.

3. Combine beef, pork, bread crumb mixture, onion, 2 tablespoons parsley, salt, allspice and pepper in large bowl; mix well. Cover; refrigerate 1 hour.

4. Pat meat mixture into 1-inch-thick square on cutting board. Cut into 36 squares. Shape each square into a ball. Melt remaining 1 tablespoon butter in same skillet over medium heat. Add meatballs. Cook 10 minutes or until browned on all sides and no longer pink in centers. Remove meatballs; drain on paper towels.

5. Drain fat but do not clean skillet. Pour broth into skillet. Heat over medium-high heat, stirring frequently and scraping up any browned bits. Reduce heat to low.

6. Combine sour cream and flour in small bowl; mix well. Stir sour cream mixture into skillet; cook 5 minutes, stirring constantly. *Do not boil.* Add meatballs; cook 5 minutes more. Sprinkle with remaining 1 tablespoon parsley.

Makes 5 to 6 servings

Swedish Meatballs

Beef Wellington

6 center-cut beef tenderloin steaks, 1 inch thick (about 2 1/2 pounds)

3/4 teaspoon salt, divided

1/2 teaspoon black pepper, divided

2 tablespoons butter or margarine

8 ounces crimini or button mushrooms, finely chopped

1/4 cup finely chopped shallots

2 tablespoons ruby port or sweet Madeira wine

1 package (17 1/4 ounces) frozen puff pastry, thawed

1 egg, separated

1/2 cup (4 ounces) purchased liver pâté*

2 teaspoons water

*Pâté can be found in the gourmet or deli section of most supermarkets or in specialty food stores.

1. Sprinkle steaks with 1/2 teaspoon salt and 1/4 teaspoon pepper. Heat large nonstick skillet over medium-high heat until hot. Cook steaks in batches about 3 minutes per side or until well browned and instant-read thermometer inserted into center of steaks registers 110°F (very rare). Transfer to plate; set aside and let cool. (If meat is tied, remove string and discard.)

2. Melt butter in same skillet over medium heat; add mushrooms and shallots. Cook and stir 5 minutes or until mushrooms are tender. Add port, remaining 1/4 teaspoon salt and 1/4 teaspoon pepper. Bring to a boil. Reduce heat; simmer 10 minutes or until liquid evaporates, stirring often. Remove from heat; cool completely.

3. Roll out each pastry sheet to 18×10-inch rectangle on lightly floured surface with lightly floured rolling pin. Cut each sheet into 3 (10×6-inch) rectangles. Cut small amount of pastry from corners to use as decoration, if desired.

4. Beat egg white in small bowl with whisk until foamy; brush over each pastry rectangle. Place 1 cooled steak on each pastry rectangle. Spread pâté over steaks, dividing evenly. Top with mushroom mixture and press lightly.

5. Carefully turn each steak over, mushroom side down. Fold pastry over steak; press edges to seal. Place on ungreased baking sheet. Cut pastry scraps into shapes and use to decorate, if desired.

6. Beat egg yolk and water in small bowl. Brush pastry with egg yolk mixture. Cover loosely with plastic wrap; refrigerate 1 to 4 hours or until cold.

7. Preheat oven to 400°F. Bake 20 to 25 minutes or until pastry is puffed and golden brown and steaks are medium (145°F). Let stand 10 minutes before serving.

Makes 6 servings

Golden Glazed Flank Steak

  1 envelope **LIPTON® RECIPE SECRETS® Onion Soup Mix***
  1 jar (12 ounces) apricot or peach preserves
1/2 cup water
  1 beef flank steak (about 2 pounds), cut into thin strips
  2 medium green, red and/or yellow bell peppers, sliced
    Hot cooked rice

Also terrific with LIPTON® RECIPE SECRETS® Onion-Mushroom Soup Mix.

1. In small bowl, combine soup mix, preserves and water; set aside.

2. On foil-lined grid or in bottom of broiler pan with rack removed, arrange steak and green peppers; top with soup mixture.

3. Grill or broil, turning steak and vegetables once, until steak is done. Serve over hot rice.

Makes 8 servings

SPAM® à la King

1/3 cup chopped green bell pepper
3 tablespoons butter or margarine
3 tablespoons all-purpose flour
1/4 teaspoon salt
1/8 teaspoon coarsely ground black pepper
1 cup water
1 cup half-and-half cream
1 HERB-OX® Chicken Flavored Bouillon Cube
1 (12-ounce) can SPAM® Classic, cubed
1 (4-ounce) can sliced mushrooms, drained
1/4 cup chopped pimiento
   Puff pastry shells, rice or toast

In large saucepan, sauté bell pepper in butter until tender. Blend in flour, salt and black pepper until smooth. Stir in water, half-and-half and bouillon cube. Cook over low heat, stirring until bouillon dissolves and mixture boils and thickens. Add SPAM®, mushrooms and pimiento. Cook and stir 3 minutes. Serve over puff pastry shells.

Makes 4 servings

helpful hint:

Hawaiians consume more SPAM® than residents of any other state in America. To combine the best of both worlds, try the SPAM™ Hawaiian Pizza on page 116, too.

SPAM® à la King

Souperior Meat Loaf

  2 pounds ground beef
  ³/₄ cup plain dry bread crumbs*
  1 envelope LIPTON® RECIPE SECRETS® Onion Soup Mix**
  ³/₄ cup water
  ¹/₃ cup ketchup
  2 eggs

Substitution: Use 1 ¹/₂ cups fresh bread crumbs or 5 slices fresh bread, cubed.

**Also terrific with LIPTON® RECIPE SECRETS® Beefy Onion, Onion Mushroom, Beefy Mushroom or Savory Herb with Garlic Soup Mix.*

1. Preheat oven to 350°F. In large bowl, combine all ingredients.

2. In 13×9-inch baking or roasting pan, shape into loaf.

3. Bake uncovered 1 hour or until done. Let stand 10 minutes before serving.

Makes 8 servings

Slow Cooker Method: In slow cooker, arrange meat. Cook covered on HIGH for 4 hours or LOW 6 to 8 hours.

Tip: Placing meat loaf on a piece of cheesecloth and then on a rack helps to hold the meat together while lifting in and out of slow cooker.

Tip: It's a snap to make fresh bread crumbs. Simply process fresh or day old white, Italian or French bread in a food processor or blender until fine crumbs form.

Prep Time: 10 minutes
Cook Time: 1 hour

Souperior Meat Loaf

Veal Scallopini

4 veal cutlets, ³⁄₈ inch thick (about **4** ounces each)
¹⁄₄ cup (¹⁄₂ stick) butter
¹⁄₂ pound fresh mushrooms, thinly sliced
2 tablespoons olive oil
1 small onion, finely chopped
¹⁄₄ cup dry sherry
2 teaspoons all-purpose flour
¹⁄₂ cup beef broth
¹⁄₄ teaspoon salt
¹⁄₈ teaspoon black pepper
2 tablespoons heavy cream or whipping cream
Hot cooked pasta

1. Pound veal with meat mallet to ¹⁄₄-inch thickness; pat dry with paper towels.

2. Heat butter in large skillet over medium heat until melted and bubbly. Cook and stir mushrooms in hot butter 3 to 4 minutes or until lightly browned. Remove mushrooms with slotted spoon; reserve.

3. Add oil to butter in skillet; heat over medium heat. Add veal; cook 2 to 3 minutes per side or until light brown. Remove veal; set aside.

4. Add onion to same skillet; cook and stir 2 to 3 minutes or until soft. Stir in sherry; boil over medium-high heat 15 seconds. Stir in flour; cook and stir 30 seconds. Stir in broth; bring to a boil over medium heat, stirring constantly. Stir in reserved mushrooms, salt and pepper. Add veal to sauce mixture; reduce heat to low. Cover; simmer 8 minutes or until veal is tender. Remove from heat.

5. Remove veal to serving plates. Stir cream into sauce mixture; mix well. Cook over low heat until heated through. Serve over pasta and veal. *Makes 4 servings*

Veal Scallopini

Beef Stroganoff

    8 ounces uncooked egg noodles
 1/4 cup all-purpose flour
 1/2 teaspoon salt
 1/4 teaspoon black pepper
1 1/4 pounds beef tenderloin steaks or tenderloin tips
    4 tablespoons butter, divided
 3/4 cup chopped onion
 12 ounces mushrooms, sliced
    1 can (10 1/2 ounces) condensed beef broth
    2 tablespoons tomato paste
    1 tablespoon Worcestershire sauce
    1 cup sour cream, at room temperature
    Fresh chives (optional)

1. Cook noodles according to package directions; drain and keep warm.

2. Meanwhile, combine flour, salt and pepper in large resealable food storage bag. Cut steaks into 1 1/2 × 1/2-inch strips; add half of beef to flour mixture. Seal bag; shake to coat well. Repeat with remaining beef. Discard flour mixture.

3. Melt 1 tablespoon butter in large nonstick skillet over medium-high heat. Add half of beef to skillet. Cook and stir until browned on all sides. *Do not overcook.* Transfer to medium bowl. Repeat with 1 tablespoon butter and remaining beef; transfer to same bowl. Set aside.

4. Melt remaining 2 tablespoons butter in same skillet over medium-high heat. Add onion; cook 5 minutes, stirring occasionally. Add mushrooms; cook and stir 5 minutes or until mushrooms are tender.

5. Stir in broth, tomato paste and Worcestershire; bring to a boil, scraping up any browned bits.

6. Return beef and any accumulated juices to skillet; cook about 5 minutes or until heated through and sauce thickens. Stir in sour cream; heat through. *Do not boil.*

7. Serve beef mixture over noodles. Garnish with chives.   *Makes 4 servings*

Beef Stroganoff

59

Boppin' Birds

Poultry certainly got the royal treatment in the '50s.

It was sauced, smothered, fricasseed and stuffed into

crêpes or cabbage. Servicemen returning from abroad

had experienced a bit of European cuisine, so stateside

cooks were ready to experiment with Chicken Cordon

Bleu or Coq au Vin. Of course, all-American birds

including Southern Buttermilk Fried Chicken, never

went out of fashion and never will.

Homestyle Chicken Pot Pie (page 70)

Manhattan Turkey à la King

- 8 ounces wide egg noodles
- 1 pound boneless turkey or chicken, cut into strips
- 1 tablespoon vegetable oil
- 1 can (14½ ounces) **DEL MONTE**® Diced Tomatoes with Garlic & Onions
- 1 can (10¾ ounces) condensed cream of celery soup
- 1 medium onion, chopped
- 2 stalks celery, sliced
- 1 cup sliced mushrooms

1. Cook noodles according to package directions; drain. In large skillet, brown turkey in oil over medium-high heat. Season with salt and pepper, if desired.

2. Add remaining ingredients, except noodles. Cover and cook over medium heat 5 minutes.

3. Remove cover; cook 5 minutes or until thickened, stirring occasionally. Serve over hot noodles. Garnish with chopped parsley, if desired.   *Makes 6 servings*

Tip: Cook pasta ahead; rinse and drain. Cover and refrigerate. Just before serving, heat in microwave or dip in boiling water.

Prep Time: 7 minutes
Cook Time: 20 minutes

Manhattan Turkey à la King

Southern Buttermilk Fried Chicken

2 cups all-purpose flour
1 ½ teaspoons celery salt
1 teaspoon dried thyme
¾ teaspoon black pepper
½ teaspoon dried marjoram
1 ¾ cups buttermilk
2 cups vegetable oil
3 pounds chicken pieces

1. Combine flour, celery salt, thyme, pepper and marjoram in shallow bowl. Pour buttermilk into medium bowl.

2. Heat oil in heavy deep skillet over medium heat until oil reaches 340°F on deep-fat thermometer.

3. Dip chicken in buttermilk, one piece at a time; shake off excess. Coat with flour mixture; shake off excess. Dip again in buttermilk, and coat once more with flour mixture. Fry chicken in batches, skin side down, 10 to 12 minutes or until browned. Turn and fry 12 to 14 minutes or until cooked through (170°F for breast meat and 180°F for dark meat). Drain on paper towels. Repeat with remaining chicken.

Makes 4 servings

Tip: Carefully monitor the temperature of the vegetable oil during cooking. It should not drop below 325°F or go higher than 350°F. Chicken may also be cooked in a deep fryer following the manufacturer's directions. Never leave hot oil unattended.

Southern Buttermilk Fried Chicken

Coq au Vin

   ¹/₂ **cup all-purpose flour**
 1 ¹/₄ **teaspoons salt**
   ³/₄ **teaspoon black pepper**
 3 ¹/₂ **pounds chicken pieces**
   2 **tablespoons butter or margarine**
   8 **ounces mushrooms, cut in half if large**
   4 **cloves garlic, minced**
   ³/₄ **cup chicken broth**
   ³/₄ **cup dry red wine**
   2 **teaspoons dried thyme**
 1 ¹/₂ **pounds red potatoes, quartered**
   2 **cups frozen pearl onions (about 8 ounces)**

1. Preheat oven to 350°F. Combine flour, salt and pepper in large resealable food storage bag. Add chicken, two pieces at a time. Seal bag; shake to coat. Repeat with remaining chicken. Reserve remaining flour mixture.

2. Melt butter in ovenproof Dutch oven over medium-high heat. Arrange chicken in single layer in Dutch oven and cook 3 minutes per side or until browned. Transfer to plate; set aside. Repeat with remaining pieces.

3. Add mushrooms and garlic to Dutch oven; cook and stir 2 minutes. Sprinkle reserved flour mixture over mushroom mixture; cook and stir 1 minute. Add broth, wine and thyme; bring to a boil over high heat, stirring to scrape up browned bits on bottom of Dutch oven. Add potatoes and onions; return to a boil. Remove from heat and add chicken, partially covering with liquid.

4. Bake, covered, about 45 minutes or until chicken is cooked through (170°F for breast meat, 180°F for dark meat) and potatoes are tender. Transfer chicken and vegetables to shallow bowls. Spoon sauce over chicken and vegetables.

Makes 4 to 6 servings

Coq au Vin

Classic Chicken Marsala

  2 tablespoons unsalted butter
  1 tablespoon vegetable oil
  4 boneless skinless chicken breasts
  4 slices mozzarella cheese (1 ounce each)
12 capers, drained
  4 flat anchovy fillets, drained
  1 tablespoon chopped fresh parsley
  1 clove garlic, minced
  3 tablespoons Marsala wine
 ⅔ cup whipping cream
    Salt and pepper
    Hot cooked pasta

1. Heat butter and oil in large skillet over medium-high heat until melted and bubbly. Add chicken; reduce heat to medium. Cook, uncovered, 5 to 6 minutes per side or until chicken is golden brown. Remove from heat. Top each chicken breast with 1 cheese slice, 3 capers and 1 anchovy fillet.

2. Return skillet to heat. Sprinkle chicken with parsley. Cover and cook over low heat 3 minutes or until cheese is melted and chicken is no longer pink in center. Remove chicken to serving dish; keep warm.

3. Add garlic to skillet; cook and stir over medium heat 30 seconds. Stir in wine; cook and stir 45 seconds, scraping up any brown bits in skillet. Stir in cream. Cook and stir 3 minutes or until sauce thickens slightly. Season with salt and pepper. Spoon sauce over chicken. Serve with pasta. *Makes 4 servings*

Classic Chicken Marsala

Homestyle Chicken Pot Pie

2 tablespoons butter, divided
1 pound boneless skinless chicken breasts, cut into 1-inch pieces
$\frac{1}{2}$ teaspoon salt
$\frac{1}{2}$ teaspoon dried thyme
$\frac{1}{4}$ teaspoon black pepper
1 package (16 ounces) frozen mixed vegetables, thawed and drained
1 can (10$\frac{3}{4}$ ounces) condensed cream of chicken or mushroom soup, undiluted
$\frac{1}{3}$ cup dry white wine or milk
1 refrigerated pie crust ($\frac{1}{2}$ of 15-ounce package), at room temperature

1. Preheat oven to 425°F. Melt 1 tablespoon butter in medium broilerproof skillet over medium-high heat. Add chicken; sprinkle with salt, thyme and pepper. Cook 1 minute, stirring frequently.

2. Reduce heat to medium-low. Stir in vegetables, soup and wine; simmer 5 minutes.

3. Meanwhile, unwrap pie crust. Using small cookie cutter, make decorative cut-outs from pastry to allow steam to escape.

4. Remove skillet from heat; top with pie crust. Melt remaining 1 tablespoon butter. Arrange cut-outs attractively over crust, if desired. Brush crust with melted butter. Bake 12 minutes. Turn oven to broil. Broil 4 to 5 inches from heat 2 minutes or until crust is golden brown and chicken mixture is bubbly. *Makes 4 to 5 servings*

Tip: If you skin and debone chicken breasts yourself, be sure to reserve both the bones and skin. Let these scraps collect in a resealable food storage bag in your freezer and soon there will be enough to make a flavorful homemade chicken stock.

Prep Time: 5 minutes
Cook Time: 25 minutes

Chicken Bourguignonne

- 4 pounds boneless skinless chicken thighs and breasts
- All-purpose flour
- Nonstick cooking spray
- 2 cups chicken broth
- 2 cups dry white wine or additional chicken broth
- 1 pound baby carrots
- $1/4$ cup tomato paste
- 4 cloves garlic, minced
- $1/2$ teaspoon dried thyme
- 2 bay leaves
- $1/4$ teaspoon salt
- $1/4$ teaspoon black pepper
- 8 ounces fresh or frozen pearl onions, thawed
- 8 ounces whole mushrooms
- 2 cups hot cooked white rice
- 2 cups hot cooked wild rice
- $1/4$ cup minced fresh parsley

1. Preheat oven to 325°F. Coat chicken very lightly with flour. Generously spray nonstick ovenproof Dutch oven or large ovenproof skillet with cooking spray; heat over medium heat. Cook chicken 10 to 15 minutes or until browned on all sides. Drain fat from Dutch oven.

2. Add chicken broth, wine, carrots, tomato paste, garlic, thyme, bay leaves, salt and pepper to Dutch oven; bring to a boil. Cover; transfer to oven. Bake 1 hour. Add onions and mushrooms. Uncover; bake about 35 minutes or until vegetables are tender and chicken is no longer pink in center. Remove and discard bay leaves. Combine white and wild rice; serve with chicken. Sprinkle with parsley.

Makes 8 servings

Chicken with Brandied Fruit Sauce

4 boneless, skinless chicken breast halves
$1/2$ teaspoon salt
$1/4$ teaspoon ground nutmeg
2 tablespoons butter or margarine
1 tablespoon cornstarch
$1/4$ teaspoon ground red pepper
  Juice of **1** orange
  Juice of **1** lemon
  Juice of **1** lime
$1/3$ cup orange marmalade
2 tablespoons brandy
1 cup red seedless grapes

Pound chicken to $1/2$-inch thickness on hard surface with meat mallet or rolling pin. Sprinkle salt and nutmeg over chicken. Heat butter in large skillet over medium-high heat. Add chicken and cook, turning, about 8 minutes or until chicken is brown and fork-tender. Mix cornstarch and red pepper in small bowl. Stir in orange juice, lemon juice and lime juice; set aside. Remove chicken to serving platter. Add marmalade to same skillet; heat until melted. Stir in juice mixture; cook and stir until mixture boils and thickens. Add brandy and grapes. Return chicken to pan; spoon sauce over chicken. Cook over low heat 5 minutes. *Makes 4 servings*

Favorite recipe from **Delmarva Poultry Industry, Inc.**

Chicken with Brandied Fruit Sauce

73

Chicken Fricassee

3 pounds chicken pieces
All-purpose flour
Nonstick cooking spray
3 cups chicken broth
1 bay leaf
1 pound baby carrots
1 medium onion, cut into wedges
1 tablespoon butter
3 tablespoons all-purpose flour
¾ cup milk
1 tablespoon lemon juice
3 tablespoons minced fresh dill *or* **2** teaspoons dried dill weed
1 teaspoon sugar
½ teaspoon salt
6 cups hot cooked noodles

1. Coat chicken pieces very lightly with flour. Spray large skillet with cooking spray; heat over medium heat. Cook chicken 10 to 15 minutes or until browned on all sides. Drain fat from skillet.

2. Add chicken broth and bay leaf to skillet; bring to a boil. Reduce heat to low and simmer, covered, about 40 minutes or until chicken is cooked through (170°F for breast meat, 180°F for dark meat). Add carrots and onion during last 20 minutes of cooking time.

3. Transfer chicken and vegetables with slotted spoon to platter; keep warm. Bring broth to a boil; boil until reduced to 1 cup. Remove and discard bay leaf.

4. Melt butter in small saucepan over low heat; stir in 3 tablespoons flour. Cook and stir 1 to 2 minutes. Stir in broth, milk and lemon juice; bring to a boil. Boil until thickened, stirring constantly. Stir in dill, sugar and salt.

5. Serve chicken and vegetables with noodles. Top with sauce.   *Makes 6 servings*

Chicken Fricassee

Boppin' Birds

Spanish Rice & Chicken Skillet

1 tablespoon oil
4 chicken drumsticks (about 1 pound)
1 onion, chopped
1/2 medium green bell pepper, chopped
1/2 medium red bell pepper, chopped
1 package (about 4 ounces) Spanish rice mix
1 can (14 1/2 ounces) diced tomatoes, undrained
1 1/4 cups chicken broth

1. Heat oil in medium skillet over high heat. Add chicken; cook 5 minutes or until lightly browned on all sides. Add onion and bell peppers; cook and stir 2 minutes.

2. Stir in rice mix, tomatoes with juice and broth. Bring to a boil. Cover and simmer over low heat 15 minutes or until rice is tender and liquid is absorbed. Remove from heat and let stand, covered, 5 minutes. *Makes 4 servings*

helpful hint:

Skillet dishes are fast and easy meals. They require just a few ingredients and only use one pan, making cleanup a breeze and leaving plenty of time to enjoy your meal.

Spanish Rice & Chicken Skillet

Chicken Cordon Bleu

  6 boneless skinless chicken breasts (about 1 ¼ pounds)
  1 tablespoon Dijon mustard
  3 slices (1 ounce each) ham, cut into halves
  3 slices (1 ounce each) Swiss cheese, cut into halves
   Nonstick cooking spray
  ¼ cup unseasoned dry bread crumbs
  2 tablespoons minced fresh parsley
  3 cups hot cooked white rice

1. Preheat oven to 350°F. Place chicken breasts between 2 sheets of plastic wrap; pound to ¼-inch thickness using flat side of meat mallet or rolling pin. Brush mustard on 1 side of each chicken breast; layer 1 slice each of ham and cheese over mustard. Roll up each chicken breast from short end; secure with toothpicks. Spray tops of chicken rolls with cooking spray; sprinkle with bread crumbs.

2. Arrange chicken rolls in 11×7-inch baking pan. Cover; bake 10 minutes. Uncover; bake about 20 minutes or until chicken is no longer pink in center. Stir parsley into rice; serve with chicken. Serve with vegetables, if desired. *Makes 6 servings*

Chicken Cordon Bleu

Chicken and Broccoli Crêpes

10 prepared Basic Crêpes (recipe follows)
$^1\!/_2$ cup all-purpose flour
$^1\!/_2$ cup half-and-half
$^1\!/_2$ teaspoon garlic salt
1 $^1\!/_4$ cups chicken broth
2 cups (8 ounces) shredded Wisconsin Cheddar cheese, divided
$^1\!/_2$ cup (2 ounces) shredded Wisconsin Monterey Jack cheese
1 $^1\!/_2$ cups dairy sour cream, divided
2 tablespoons diced pimiento
1 tablespoon parsley flakes
1 teaspoon paprika
2 tablespoons butter
1 can (4 ounces) sliced mushrooms, drained
2 packages (10 ounces each) frozen broccoli spears, cooked and drained
2 cups cubed cooked chicken

Prepare Basic Crêpes; set aside. Combine flour, half-and-half and garlic salt in medium saucepan; beat with wire whisk until smooth. Blend in chicken broth. Stir in 1 cup Cheddar cheese, Monterey Jack cheese, $^1\!/_2$ cup sour cream, pimiento, parsley and paprika. Cook sauce over medium-low heat until mixture thickens, stirring constantly. Remove from heat; set aside. Melt butter in small skillet over medium-high heat. Cook and stir mushrooms in butter.

On half of each crêpe, place equally divided portions of cooked broccoli, chicken and mushrooms. Spoon 1 to 2 tablespoons cheese sauce over each.

Fold crêpes. Place in large, shallow baking dish. Pour remaining cheese sauce over crêpes. Top with remaining 1 cup sour cream and 1 cup Cheddar cheese. Bake, uncovered, in preheated 350°F oven 5 to 10 minutes or until cheese melts. Garnish with chopped fresh parsley, if desired.   *Makes 10 crêpes*

Favorite recipe from **Wisconsin Milk Marketing Board**

Basic Crêpes

3 eggs
$1/2$ **teaspoon salt**
2 cups plus 2 tablespoons all-purpose flour
2 cups milk
$1/4$ **cup melted butter**

Beat eggs and salt together in medium bowl with electric mixer or wire whisk. Add flour alternately with milk, beating until smooth. Stir in melted butter.

Allow crêpe batter to stand 1 hour or more in refrigerator before cooking. The flour may expand and bubbles will collapse. The batter should be the consistency of heavy cream. If the batter is too thick, add 1 to 2 tablespoons additional milk and stir well.

Cook crêpes in heated, nonstick pan over medium-high heat. With one hand, pour 3 tablespoons batter into pan; with other hand, lift pan off heat. Quickly rotate pan until batter covers bottom; return pan to heat. Cook until light brown; turn and brown other side for a few seconds.   *Makes about 30 crêpes*

Note: To store crêpes, separate with pieces of waxed paper and wrap airtight. They may be frozen for up to 3 months.

Favorite recipe from **Wisconsin Milk Marketing Board**

Chicken Breasts Smothered in Tomatoes and Mozzarella

    4 boneless skinless chicken breasts (about 1 $\frac{1}{2}$ pounds)
    3 tablespoons olive oil, divided
    1 cup chopped onions
    2 teaspoons minced garlic
    1 can (about 14 ounces) Italian-style stewed tomatoes
  1 $\frac{1}{2}$ cups (**6 ounces**) shredded mozzarella cheese

1. Preheat broiler.

2. Pound chicken breasts between 2 pieces of plastic wrap to $\frac{1}{4}$-inch thickness using flat side of meat mallet or rolling pin.

3. Heat 2 tablespoons oil in ovenproof skillet over medium heat. Add chicken; cook about 3$\frac{1}{2}$ minutes per side or until no longer pink in center. Transfer to plate; cover and keep warm.

4. Heat remaining 1 tablespoon oil in same skillet over medium heat. Add onions and garlic; cook and stir 3 minutes. Add tomatoes; bring to a simmer. Return chicken to skillet; spoon onion and tomato mixture over chicken.

5. Sprinkle cheese over top. Broil 4 to 5 inches from heat until cheese is melted.

Makes 4 servings

Prep and Cook Time: 20 minutes

Chicken Breast Smothered in Tomatoes and Mozzarella

Chicken with Peach-Champagne Sauce

CHICKEN

- 1 whole chicken breast, split, boned and skinned
- 2 teaspoons lemon juice
   Pepper to taste
- 2 fresh California peaches, sliced

PEACH-CHAMPAGNE SAUCE

- 1 tablespoon margarine or butter
- 1 tablespoon minced red onion
- 1 tablespoon all-purpose flour
- $1/3$ cup champagne or white wine
   Spinach noodles, cooked (optional)

MICROWAVE DIRECTIONS

For Chicken, in small microwave-safe baking dish, arrange chicken, with meatiest parts toward edges of dish. Sprinkle with lemon juice and pepper. Cover with wax paper and microwave on HIGH 5 minutes or until cooked through and no longer pink in center; reserve cooking liquid. Add peach slices to chicken and cook on HIGH 1 to 2 minutes longer.

For Sauce, in 4-cup glass measure, combine margarine and onion. Cook on HIGH 1 minute. Stir in flour and 3 tablespoons cooking liquid. Stir in champagne. Cook on HIGH 3 minutes or until thickened, stirring after 1 1/2 minutes. Serve chicken and peaches on noodles. Spoon sauce over chicken.   *Makes 2 servings*

Favorite recipe from **California Tree Fruit Agreement**

Chicken with Peach-Champagne Sauce

Chicken Wellington

6 large boneless skinless chicken breasts
$3/4$ teaspoon salt, divided
$1/4$ teaspoon black pepper, divided
4 tablespoons butter, divided
1 2 ounces mushrooms, finely chopped
$1/2$ cup finely chopped shallots or onion
2 tablespoons port wine or cognac
1 tablespoon fresh thyme *or* 1 teaspoon dried thyme, crushed
1 package (1 7 $1/4$ ounces) frozen puff pastry, thawed
1 egg, separated
1 tablespoon Dijon mustard
1 teaspoon milk

1. Sprinkle chicken with $1/4$ teaspoon salt and $1/8$ teaspoon pepper. Melt 2 tablespoons butter in large skillet over medium heat. Brown chicken breasts in batches 6 minutes, turning once. Transfer to plate; cool slightly.

2. Melt remaining 2 tablespoons butter in skillet over medium heat. Add mushrooms and shallots. Cook and stir 5 minutes or until mushrooms release their liquid. Add wine, thyme, remaining $1/2$ teaspoon salt and $1/8$ teaspoon pepper; simmer until liquid evaporates, stirring often. Cool.

3. Roll out each pastry sheet to 15×12-inch rectangle. Cut into 3 rectangles, 12×5 inches each. Cut small amount of pastry from corners into decorative shapes. Brush beaten egg white over pastry rectangles. Place 1 cooled chicken breast on one side of each pastry rectangle. Spread $1/2$ teaspoon mustard over each chicken breast, then spread with $1/4$ cup mushroom mixture. Fold pastry over chicken; press edges to seal. Place on ungreased baking sheet; top with pastry shapes. Whisk combined egg yolk and milk in small bowl; brush over pastry. Cover loosely with plastic wrap. Refrigerate until cold, 1 to 4 hours.

4. Preheat oven to 400°F. Bake 25 to 30 minutes or until chicken is 170°F and pastry is deep golden brown. *Makes 6 servings*

Chicken Wellington

Cruisin' Casseroles

Did casseroles exist before the '50s? Of course, but

this was the decade that turned them into the ultimate

comfort food. Now homemakers had canned soups and

vegetables to radically cut down on preparation time,

so casseroles became as easy as (chicken pot) pie.

Whether it was turning a can of salmon into Friday night

dinner, or impressing the neighbors with a buffet

featuring Chicken Tetrazzini, casseroles were king.

Hearty Shepherd's Pie (page 97)

Salmon Casserole

2 tablespoons butter
2 cups sliced mushrooms
1 ½ cups chopped carrots
1 cup frozen peas
1 cup chopped celery
½ cup chopped onion
½ cup chopped red bell pepper
1 tablespoon chopped fresh parsley
1 clove garlic, minced
1 teaspoon salt
½ teaspoon black pepper
½ teaspoon dried basil
4 cups cooked rice
1 can (14 ounces) red salmon, drained and flaked
1 can (10¾ ounces) condensed cream of mushroom soup, undiluted
2 cups (8 ounces) shredded Cheddar or American cheese
½ cup sliced black olives

1. Preheat oven to 350°F. Spray 2-quart casserole with nonstick cooking spray.

2. Melt butter in large skillet or Dutch oven over medium heat. Add mushrooms, carrots, peas, celery, onion, bell pepper, parsley, garlic, salt, black pepper and basil; cook and stir 10 minutes or until vegetables are tender. Add rice, salmon, soup and cheese; mix well.

3. Transfer to prepared casserole; sprinkle with olives. Bake 30 minutes or until hot and bubbly.   *Makes 8 servings*

Salmon Casserole

Cruisin' Casseroles

Classic Turkey Pot Pie

  2 cans (15 ounces each) VEG•ALL® Original Mixed Vegetables, drained
  1 can (10¾ ounces) cream of potato soup, undiluted
¼ cup milk
  1 pound cooked turkey, shredded (2 cups)
¼ teaspoon dried thyme
¼ teaspoon black pepper
  2 (9-inch) refrigerated ready-to-bake pie crusts

Preheat oven to 375°F. In medium mixing bowl, combine first 6 ingredients; mix well. Place 1 pie crust into 9-inch pie pan; pour vegetable mixture into pie crust. Top with remaining crust, crimp edges to seal, and slit top with knife. Bake for 50 to 60 minutes (on lower rack) or until crust is golden brown and filling is hot. Allow pie to cool slightly before cutting into wedges to serve.   *Makes 8 servings*

Crunchy Veg•All® Tuna Casserole

  2 cups cooked medium egg noodles
  1 can (15 ounces) VEG•ALL® Original Mixed Vegetables, drained
  1 can (12 ounces) solid white tuna in water, drained
  1 can (10.75 ounces) cream of celery soup, undrained
1¼ cups whole milk
½ cup sour cream
  1 tablespoon chopped fresh dill
  1 cup crushed sour cream & onion potato chips

Combine all ingredients except potato chips in greased 1½-quart casserole dish.

Microwave, uncovered, on High for 10 to 12 minutes or until very thick. Let cool for 10 minutes.

Top with crushed potato chips and serve.   *Makes 4 to 6 servings*

Classic Turkey Pot Pie

Cheeseburger Macaroni

1 cup mostaccioli or elbow macaroni, uncooked
1 pound ground beef
1 medium onion, chopped
1 can (14½ ounces) **DEL MONTE**® Diced Tomatoes with Basil, Garlic & Oregano
¼ cup **DEL MONTE**® Tomato Ketchup
1 cup (**4 ounces**) shredded Cheddar cheese

1. Cook pasta according to package directions; drain.

2. Brown meat with onion in large skillet; drain. Season with salt and pepper, if desired. Stir in undrained tomatoes, ketchup and pasta; heat through.

3. Top with cheese. Garnish, if desired.   *Makes 4 servings*

Prep Time: 8 minutes
Cook Time: 15 minutes

SPAM™ Cornbread Pie

1 (8½-ounce) package cornbread mix
1 (12-ounce) can **SPAM**® Classic, cubed
1½ cups (**6 ounces**) shredded Cheddar cheese

Heat oven to 400°F. Prepare cornbread mix according to package directions. Stir in SPAM®. Spread in 9-inch greased pie plate. Bake 15 to 20 minutes. Sprinkle with cheese. Bake 5 to 10 minutes or until cornbread is done.   *Makes 6 servings*

Cheeseburger Macaroni

95

★ Cruisin'★ Casseroles

Scalloped Garlic Potatoes

3 medium all-purpose potatoes, peeled and thinly sliced (about 1 ½ pounds)
1 envelope **LIPTON® RECIPE SECRETS®** Savory Herb with Garlic Soup Mix
1 cup (½ pint) whipping or heavy cream
½ cup water

1. Preheat oven to 375°F. In lightly greased 2-quart shallow baking dish, arrange potatoes. In medium bowl, blend remaining ingredients; pour over potatoes.

2. Bake, uncovered, 45 minutes or until potatoes are tender.   *Makes 4 servings*

Veg•All® Beef & Cheddar Bake

2 cans (15 ounces each) **VEG•ALL®** Original Mixed Vegetables, drained
3 cups shredded Cheddar cheese
2 cups cooked elbow macaroni
1 pound extra-lean ground beef, cooked and drained
½ cup chopped onion
¼ teaspoon black pepper

1. Preheat oven to 350°F.

2. In large mixing bowl, combine Veg•All, cheese, macaroni, ground beef, onion and pepper; mix well. Pour mixture into large casserole.

3. Bake for 30 to 35 minutes. Serve hot.   *Makes 4 to 6 servings*

Hearty Shephend's Pie

1 ½ **pounds ground beef**
  2 **cups** *French's*® **French Fried Onions**
  1 **can (**10¾ **ounces) condensed tomato soup**
½ **cup water**
  2 **teaspoons Italian seasoning**
¼ **teaspoon each salt and black pepper**
  1 **package (**10 **ounces) frozen mixed vegetables, thawed**
  3 **cups hot mashed potatoes**

1. Preheat oven to 375°F. Cook meat in large oven-proof skillet until browned; drain. Stir in *1 cup* French Fried Onions, soup, water, seasoning, salt and pepper.

2. Spoon vegetables over beef mixture. Top with mashed potatoes.

3. Bake 20 minutes or until hot. Sprinkle with remaining *1 cup* onions. Bake 2 minutes or until golden.

Makes 6 servings

Prep Time: 10 minutes
Cook Time: 27 minutes

Scalloped Apples & Onions

1 medium onion, thinly sliced
4 tablespoons butter, melted, divided
5 red or green apples, cored and thinly sliced
8 ounces (1 ½ cups) pasteurized process cheese, cut into small pieces, divided
2 cups *French's*® French Fried Onions, divided

1. Preheat oven to 375°F. Sauté onion in 2 tablespoons butter in medium skillet over medium-high heat 3 minutes or until tender. Add apples and sauté 5 minutes or until apples are tender.

2. Stir 1 cup cheese, *1 cup* French Fried Onions and remaining melted butter into apple mixture. Transfer to greased 9-inch deep-dish pie plate.

3. Bake, uncovered, 20 minutes or until heated through. Top with remaining cheese and onions. Bake 5 minutes or until cheese is melted. *Makes 6 side-dish servings*

Tip: To save time and cleanup, apple mixture may be baked in a heatproof skillet if desired. Wrap skillet handle in heavy-duty foil.

Variation: For added Cheddar flavor, substitute *French's*® *Cheddar French Fried Onions* for the original flavor.

Prep Time: 15 minutes
Cook Time: about 30 minutes

Scalloped Apples & Onions

Chicken Divan Casserole

1 cup uncooked rice
1 cup coarsely shredded carrots
   Nonstick cooking spray
4 boneless skinless chicken breasts
2 tablespoons butter
3 tablespoons all-purpose flour
$\frac{1}{4}$ teaspoon salt
   Black pepper
1 cup chicken broth
$\frac{1}{2}$ cup milk or half-and-half
$\frac{1}{4}$ cup dry white wine
$\frac{1}{3}$ cup plus 2 tablespoons grated Parmesan cheese, divided
1 pound frozen broccoli florets

1. Preheat oven to 350°F. Lightly grease 12×8-inch baking dish.

2. Prepare rice according to package directions. Stir in carrots. Spread mixture into prepared baking dish.

3. Spray large skillet with cooking spray. Heat over medium-high heat. Brown chicken breasts about 2 minutes on each side. Arrange over rice.

4. To prepare sauce, melt butter in 2-quart saucepan over medium heat. Whisk in flour, salt and pepper to taste; cook and stir 1 minute. Gradually whisk in broth and milk. Cook and stir until mixture comes to a boil. Reduce heat; simmer 2 minutes. Stir in wine. Remove from heat. Stir in $\frac{1}{3}$ cup cheese.

5. Arrange broccoli around chicken. Pour sauce over top. Sprinkle remaining 2 tablespoons cheese over chicken.

6. Cover with foil; bake 30 minutes. Remove foil; bake 10 to 15 minutes or until chicken is no longer pink in center and broccoli is hot. *Makes 6 servings*

Chicken Divan Casserole

Beef Stroganoff Casserole

1 pound ground beef

¼ teaspoon salt

⅛ teaspoon black pepper

1 teaspoon vegetable oil

8 ounces sliced mushrooms

1 large onion, chopped

3 cloves garlic, minced

¼ cup dry white wine

1 can (10¾ ounces) condensed cream of mushroom soup, undiluted

½ cup sour cream

1 tablespoon Dijon mustard

4 cups cooked egg noodles

Chopped fresh parsley (optional)

1. Preheat oven to 350°F. Spray 13×9-inch baking dish with nonstick cooking spray.

2. Place beef in large skillet; season with salt and pepper. Brown beef over medium-high heat until no longer pink, stirring to break up meat. Drain fat, remove beef from skillet and set aside.

3. Heat oil in same skillet over medium-high heat. Add mushrooms, onion and garlic; cook and stir 2 minutes or until onion is tender. Add wine. Reduce heat to medium-low and simmer 3 minutes. Remove from heat; stir in soup, sour cream and mustard until well blended. Return beef to skillet; stir to blend.

4. Place noodles in prepared dish. Pour beef mixture over noodles; stir until noodles are well coated. Bake, uncovered, 30 minutes or until heated through. Sprinkle with parsley.

Makes 6 servings

Beef Stroganoff Casserole

Country Sausage Macaroni and Cheese

- 1 pound **BOB EVANS®** Special Seasonings Roll Sausage
- 1 1/2 cups milk
- 12 ounces pasteurized processed Cheddar cheese, cut into cubes
- 1/2 cup Dijon mustard
- 1 cup diced fresh or drained canned tomatoes
- 1 cup sliced mushrooms
- 1/3 cup sliced green onions
- 1/8 teaspoon cayenne pepper
- 12 ounces uncooked elbow macaroni
- 2 tablespoons grated Parmesan cheese

Preheat oven to 350°F. Crumble and cook sausage in medium skillet until browned. Drain on paper towels. Combine milk, processed cheese and mustard in medium saucepan; cook and stir over low heat until cheese melts and mixture is smooth. Stir in sausage, tomatoes, mushrooms, green onions and cayenne pepper. Remove from heat.

Cook macaroni according to package directions; drain. Combine hot macaroni and cheese mixture in large bowl; toss until well coated. Spoon into greased shallow 2-quart casserole dish. Cover and bake 15 to 20 minutes. Stir; sprinkle with Parmesan cheese. Bake, uncovered, 5 minutes more. Let stand 10 minutes before serving. Refrigerate leftovers.   *Makes 6 to 8 servings*

Tamale Pie

    1 tablespoon BERTOLLI® Olive Oil
    1 small onion, chopped
    1 pound ground beef
    1 envelope LIPTON® RECIPE SECRETS® Onion Soup Mix*
    1 can (14½ ounces) stewed tomatoes, undrained
    ½ cup water
    1 can (15 to 19 ounces) red kidney beans, rinsed and drained
    1 package (8½ ounces) corn muffin mix

Also terrific with LIPTON® RECIPE SECRETS® Fiesta Herb with Red Pepper, Onion Mushroom, Beefy Onion or Beefy Mushroom Soup Mix.

1. Preheat oven to 400°F.

2. In 12-inch skillet, heat oil over medium heat and cook onion, stirring occasionally, 3 minutes or until tender. Stir in ground beef and cook until browned.

3. Stir in soup mix blended with tomatoes and water. Bring to a boil over high heat, stirring with spoon to crush tomatoes. Reduce heat to low and stir in beans. Simmer uncovered, stirring occasionally, 10 minutes. Turn into 2-quart casserole.

4. Prepare corn muffin mix according to package directions. Spoon evenly over casserole.

5. Bake uncovered 15 minutes or until corn topping is golden and filling is hot.

Makes 6 servings

Chicken Tetrazzini

  8 ounces uncooked vermicelli, broken in half
  1 can (10¾ ounces) condensed cream of mushroom soup, undiluted
  ¼ cup half-and-half
  3 tablespoons dry sherry
  ½ teaspoon salt
  ⅛ teaspoon red pepper flakes
  2 cups chopped cooked chicken breasts (about ¾ pound)
  1 cup frozen peas
  ½ cup grated Parmesan cheese
  1 cup fresh coarse bread crumbs
  2 tablespoons butter, melted
    Chopped fresh basil (optional)

1. Preheat oven to 375°F. Spray 8-inch square baking dish with nonstick cooking spray. Set aside.

2. Cook pasta according to package directions. Drain and set aside.

3. Meanwhile, combine soup, half-and-half, sherry, salt and red pepper flakes in large bowl. Stir in chicken, peas and cheese. Add pasta to chicken mixture; stir until pasta is well coated. Pour into prepared dish.

4. Combine bread crumbs and butter in small bowl. Sprinkle evenly over casserole. Bake, uncovered, 25 to 30 minutes or until heated through and crumbs are golden brown. Sprinkle with basil.   *Makes 4 servings*

Tip: Have rotisserie chicken from your local supermarket for dinner one night and use 2 cups leftover chicken to make Tetrazzini the next.

Chicken Tetrazzini

Seafood Newburg Casserole

1 can (10¾ ounces) condensed cream of shrimp soup, undiluted

½ cup half-and-half

1 tablespoon dry sherry

¼ teaspoon ground red pepper

2 cans (6 ounces each) lump crabmeat, drained

3 cups cooked rice

¼ pound medium raw shrimp, peeled and deveined

¼ pound raw bay scallops

1 jar (4 ounces) pimientos, drained and chopped

¼ cup finely chopped fresh parsley

1. Preheat oven to 350°F. Spray 2½-quart casserole with nonstick cooking spray.

2. Whisk together soup, half-and-half, sherry and red pepper in large bowl until blended. Pick out any shell or cartilage from crabmeat; add crabmeat, rice, shrimp, scallops and pimientos; toss well.

3. Transfer mixture to prepared casserole; cover and bake about 25 minutes or until shrimp and scallops are opaque. Sprinkle with parsley.   *Makes 6 servings*

Seafood Newburg Casserole

109

Hungarian Goulash Casserole

  1 **pound ground pork**
  1/4 **teaspoon salt**
  1/4 **teaspoon ground nutmeg**
  1/4 **teaspoon black pepper**
  1 **tablespoon vegetable oil**
  1 **cup sour cream, divided**
  1 **tablespoon cornstarch**
  1 **can (10¾ ounces) cream of celery soup, undiluted**
  1 **cup milk**
  1 **teaspoon sweet Hungarian paprika**
  1 **package (12 ounces) egg noodles, cooked and drained**
  2 **teaspoons minced fresh dill (optional)**

1. Preheat oven to 325°F. Spray 3-quart casserole dish with nonstick cooking spray.

2. Combine pork, salt, nutmeg and pepper in medium bowl. Shape into 1-inch balls. Heat oil in large skillet over medium-high heat. Add meatballs; cook 10 minutes or until browned on all sides and no longer pink in center. Remove meatballs from skillet; discard drippings.

3. Stir together ¼ cup sour cream and cornstarch in small bowl. Spoon into same skillet. Add remaining ¾ cup sour cream, soup, milk and paprika. Stir until smooth.

4. Spread cooked noodles in prepared dish. Arrange meatballs over noodles and cover with sauce. Bake 20 minutes or until hot. Sprinkle with dill.   *Make 4 to 6 servings*

Hungarian Goulash Casserole

Chicken, Asparagus & Mushroom Bake

1 tablespoon butter

1 tablespoon olive oil

2 boneless skinless chicken breasts (about $1/2$ pound), cut into bite-size pieces

2 cloves garlic, minced

1 cup sliced mushrooms

2 cups sliced asparagus

  Black pepper

1 package (about 6 ounces) corn bread stuffing mix

$1/4$ cup dry white wine (optional)

1 can (about $14^1/2$ ounces) chicken broth

1 can ($10^3/4$ ounces) condensed cream of asparagus or
    cream of chicken soup, undiluted

1. Preheat oven to 350°F. Heat butter and oil in large skillet until butter is melted. Add chicken and garlic; cook and stir about 3 minutes over medium-high heat or until chicken is no longer pink. Add mushrooms; cook and stir 2 minutes. Add asparagus; cook and stir about 5 minutes or until asparagus is crisp-tender. Season with pepper.

2. Transfer mixture to $2^1/2$-quart casserole or 6 small casseroles. Top with stuffing.

3. Add wine to skillet, if desired; cook and stir 1 minute over medium-high heat, scraping up any browned bits from bottom of skillet. Add broth and soup; cook and stir until well blended.

4. Pour broth mixture into casserole; mix well. Bake, uncovered, about 35 minutes (30 minutes for small casseroles) or until heated through and lightly browned.

Makes 6 servings

Tip: This is a good way to stretch a little leftover chicken into an easy and tasty dinner. Serve with tossed green salad and sliced tomatoes.

Chicken, Asparagus & Mushroom Bake

Luscious Luau

South Seas fever hit America hard in the '50s.

Restaurants featured frowning tiki gods and burning

torches, and everyone had to try a hula hoop at least

once. The luau was a popular theme for parties and food

usually included pineapple and coconut. So get out the

mai tai mix and experience a bit of island dreaming

yourself. From Hawaiian Ribs to Tropical Luau cupcakes,

these recipes will make you feel like doing the hula.

Tidal Wave Cocoa Almond Mousse (page 128)

Luscious Luau

SPAM™ Hawaiian Pizza

- 1 (10-ounce) can refrigerated pizza crust
- 1 (6-ounce) package sliced provolone cheese
- 1 (12-ounce) can **SPAM®** Classic, cut into thin squares
- 1 (8-ounce) can chunk pineapple, drained
- $\frac{1}{2}$ cup thinly sliced red onion rings
- $\frac{1}{2}$ cup chopped green bell pepper

Heat oven to 425°F. Grease 12-inch pizza pan or 13×9-inch baking pan. Unroll dough; press into prepared pan. Top with cheese. Arrange remaining ingredients over cheese. Bake 25 to 30 minutes or until crust is deep golden brown.

Makes 6 servings

Pineapple-Ginger Shrimp Cocktail

- 9 fresh pineapple spears, divided
- $\frac{1}{4}$ cup apricot fruit spread
- 1 tablespoon finely chopped onion
- $\frac{1}{2}$ teaspoon grated fresh ginger
- $\frac{1}{8}$ teaspoon black pepper
- $\frac{1}{2}$ pound medium cooked shrimp (about 32)
- 1 medium red or green bell pepper, cut into 12 strips

1. Chop 3 pineapple spears into bite-size pieces; combine with preserves, onion, ginger and black pepper in medium bowl.

2. Arrange shrimp, bell pepper strips and remaining pineapple spears on 6 plates or in 6 cocktail glasses. Top with pineapple mixture.

Makes 6 servings

SPAM™ Hawaiian Pizza

Chunky Hawaiian Spread

  1 package (3 ounces) light cream cheese, softened
  1/2 cup fat free or light sour cream
  1 can (8 ounces) DOLE® Crushed Pineapple, well drained
  1/4 cup mango chutney*
     Low fat crackers

*If there are large pieces of fruit in chutney, cut them into small pieces.

• Beat cream cheese, sour cream, crushed pineapple and chutney in bowl until blended. Cover and chill 1 hour or overnight. Serve with crackers. Refrigerate any leftover spread in airtight container for up to one week.   *Makes 2 1/2 cups spread*

Creamy Coconut-Lime Fruit Salad

  1/2 cup sour cream
  1/2 cup unsweetened coconut milk
  2 tablespoons lime juice
  2 tablespoons packed brown sugar
  2 seedless oranges, peeled and sectioned
  2 Granny Smith apples, cored and chopped
  2 nectarines, pitted and sliced
  1 mango, peeled, pitted and diced
  1 cup strawberry halves

Combine sour cream, coconut milk, lime juice and brown sugar in small bowl; stir until smooth. Gently toss remaining ingredients in large bowl. Pour sour cream mixture over fruit. Toss to coat well. Serve immediately or cover and refrigerate up to 4 hours.

Makes 6 to 8 servings

Chunky Hawaiian Spread

Caribbean Fruited Pork Roast

1 cup chopped mixed dried fruits

1/4 cup dry sherry

1 tablespoon *Frank's® RedHot®* Original Cayenne Pepper Sauce

1/2 teaspoon ground allspice

3 tablespoons chopped almonds

1 boneless center pork loin roast (about 3 pounds)

SPICY GLAZE & SAUCE

1 can (6 ounces) frozen apple juice concentrate, thawed

1/4 cup *Frank's® RedHot®* Original Cayenne Pepper Sauce

1 tablespoon grated peeled fresh ginger

2 teaspoons ground cumin

2 teaspoons instant coffee granules

2 teaspoons cornstarch dissolved in 1 tablespoon water

1 can (8 ounces) tomato sauce

1. Combine fruits, sherry, *Frank's RedHot* Sauce and allspice in small saucepan. Bring to a boil. Remove from heat; let stand 10 minutes. Stir in almonds.

2. Preheat oven to 350°F. With long sharp knife, make deep cut in center of each end of roast; enlarge pocket with handle of wooden spoon. Stuff fruit mixture into each opening, using handle of spoon to push filling into center. Place roast, fat side up, in greased and foil-lined roasting pan. Bake 30 minutes.

3. Combine juice concentrate, *Frank's RedHot* Sauce, ginger, cumin, coffee granules and cornstarch mixture in small saucepan. Bring to a boil over medium heat. Reduce heat to low; cook 1 minute or until thickened, stirring often. Pour 1/2 cup glaze into small bowl; reserve. Add tomato sauce to remaining glaze in saucepan. Cook, stirring, until heated through; set aside.

4. Brush reserved glaze over entire roast. Bake 45 minutes or internal temperature registers 160°F on meat thermometer inserted in thickest part of roast. Let stand 15 minutes. Slice; serve with sauce. *Makes 8 servings*

Caribbean Fruited Pork Roast

Luscious Luau

Ambrosia

- 1 can (20 ounces) DOLE® Pineapple Chunks
- 1 can (11 or 15 ounces) DOLE® Mandarin Oranges
- 1 firm, large DOLE® Banana, sliced (optional)
- 1 ½ cups DOLE® Seedless Grapes
- 1 cup miniature marshmallows
- 1 cup flaked coconut
- ½ cup pecan halves or coarsely chopped nuts
- 1 cup vanilla yogurt or sour cream
- 1 tablespoon brown sugar

• Drain pineapple chunks and mandarin oranges. In large bowl, combine pineapple chunks, mandarin oranges, banana, grapes, marshmallows, coconut and nuts. In 1-quart measure, combine yogurt and brown sugar. Stir into fruit mixture. Refrigerate, covered, 1 hour or overnight.　　　　　　　　　　　　　*Makes 4 servings*

helpful hint:

When shopping for coconut, look for sweetened flaked or shredded varieties found in the baking aisle in cans or bags. When measuring, do not pack the coconut into the spoon or cup.

Ambrosia

Spiced Grilled Bananas

  3 large ripe firm bananas
  $^1/_4$ **cup golden raisins**
  3 tablespoons packed brown sugar
  $^1/_2$ **teaspoon ground cinnamon**
  $^1/_4$ **teaspoon ground nutmeg**
  $^1/_4$ **teaspoon ground cardamom or coriander**
  2 tablespoons butter, cut into 8 pieces
  1 tablespoon fresh lime juice
     Vanilla frozen yogurt (optional)
     Additional fresh lime juice (optional)

1. Spray grillproof 9-inch pie plate with nonstick cooking spray. Cut bananas diagonally into $^1/_2$-inch-thick slices. Arrange, overlapping, in prepared pie plate. Sprinkle with raisins.

2. Combine sugar, cinnamon, nutmeg and cardamom in small bowl; sprinkle over bananas and raisins and dot with butter. Cover pie plate tightly with foil. Place on grid and grill, covered, over low coals 10 to 15 minutes or until bananas are hot and tender.

3. Carefully remove foil and sprinkle with 1 tablespoon lime juice. Serve over frozen yogurt and sprinkle with additional lime juice.

Makes 4 servings

Spiced Grilled Bananas

125

South Seas Shrimp & Mango

1 pound jumbo raw shrimp, peeled and deveined

3 tablespoons *French's®* Honey Dijon Mustard

2 tablespoons olive oil

2 tablespoons fresh orange juice

1 tablespoon *Frank's® RedHot®* Original Cayenne Pepper Sauce

1 teaspoon grated orange peel

1 large ripe mango, peeled and cut into 1-inch pieces

1 red bell pepper, cut into 1-inch pieces

4 green onions, cut into 1 1/2-inch pieces

1. Place shrimp in large resealable plastic food storage bag. Combine mustard, oil, juice, *Frank's RedHot* Sauce and orange peel in small bowl; pour over shrimp. Seal bag; marinate in refrigerator 20 minutes.

2. Alternately thread shrimp, mango, bell pepper and onions onto 4 (10-inch) metal skewers. Place skewers on oiled grid. Grill over high heat 7 minutes or until shrimp are opaque, turning and basting once with mustard mixture. Discard any remaining marinade.

Makes 4 servings

Prep Time: 15 minutes
Marinate Time: 20 minutes
Cook Time: 7 minutes

South Seas Shrimp & Mango

Tidal Wave Cocoa Almond Mousse

²/₃ cup sugar

$^2/_3$ cup sugar

$^1/_3$ cup **HERSHEY'S** Cocoa

1 envelope unflavored gelatin

1 $^1/_2$ cups (12-ounce can) evaporated nonfat milk

$^1/_2$ teaspoon almond extract

1 envelope (1.3 ounces) dry whipped topping mix

$^1/_2$ cup cold nonfat milk

$^1/_2$ teaspoon vanilla extract

1. Stir together sugar, cocoa and gelatin in medium saucepan; stir in evaporated milk until blended. Let stand 1 minute to soften gelatin. Cook over low heat, stirring constantly, until gelatin is completely dissolved, about 5 minutes.

2. Remove from heat; pour mixture into large bowl. Stir in almond extract. Refrigerate, stirring occasionally, until mixture mounds slightly when dropped from spoon.

3. Prepare topping mix as directed on package, using $^1/_2$ cup milk and $^1/_2$ teaspoon vanilla. Reserve $^1/_2$ cup topping for garnish (cover and refrigerate until ready to use); fold remaining topping into chocolate mixture. Let stand a few minutes; spoon into 7 individual dessert dishes. Cover; refrigerate until firm. Garnish with reserved topping.

Makes 7 servings

Tropical Pork Chops

1 can (8 ounces) pineapple chunks in juice
1 tablespoon cornstarch
$1/2$ cup prepared sweet and sour sauce
$1/3$ cup raisins
2 tablespoons packed brown sugar
1 tablespoon vegetable oil
4 boneless pork loin chops, $1/2$ inch thick (about 5 ounces each)
Hot cooked couscous or rice

1. Drain pineapple, reserving juice. Blend juice with cornstarch in medium bowl. Stir in pineapple, sweet and sour sauce, raisins and brown sugar; set aside.

2. Heat oil in large skillet until hot. Add chops and brown on both sides; drain excess fat. Pour pineapple mixture over pork. Cover; simmer 10 minutes or until chops are barely pink in center. Serve chops with sauce and couscous.   *Makes 4 servings*

Hawaiian Ribs

>   1 can (8 ounces) crushed pineapple in juice, undrained
> 1/3 cup apricot jam
>   3 tablespoons *French's*® Classic Yellow® Mustard
>   1 tablespoon red wine vinegar
>   2 teaspoons grated peeled fresh ginger
>   1 clove garlic, minced
>   3 to 4 pounds pork baby back ribs*

*Or, if baby back ribs are not available, substitute 4 pounds pork spareribs, cut in half lengthwise. Cut spareribs into 3- to 4-rib portions. Cook 20 minutes in enough boiling water to cover. Grill ribs 30 to 40 minutes or until no longer pink near bone, brushing with portion of pineapple mixture during last 10 minutes.

1. Combine crushed pineapple with juice, apricot jam, mustard, vinegar, ginger and garlic in blender or food processor. Cover and process until very smooth.

2. Place ribs on oiled grid. Grill ribs over medium heat 40 minutes or until ribs are no longer pink near bone. Brush ribs with portion of pineapple sauce mixture during last 10 minutes of cooking. Cut into individual ribs to serve. Serve remaining sauce for dipping.   *Makes 8 servings (1 1/2 cups sauce)*

Tip: Try mixing 2 tablespoons *French's*® Mustard, any flavor, with 3/4 cup peach-apricot sweet 'n' sour sauce to create a delicious luau fruit dip. Serve with assorted cut-up fresh fruit.

Prep Time: 10 minutes
Cook Time: 40 minutes

Hawaiian Ribs

131

Hula Chicken Salad with Orange Poppy Seed Dressing

1/2 cup prepared vinaigrette salad dressing

1/4 cup *French's*® Honey Dijon Mustard

1 tablespoon grated orange peel

1 tablespoon water

1 teaspoon poppy seeds

1 pound chicken tenders

1 tablespoon jerk seasoning

8 cups cut-up romaine lettuce

3 cups cut-up fruit from salad bar such as oranges, melon, strawberries, pineapple

1. Combine salad dressing, mustard, orange peel, water and poppy seeds; mix well. Reserve.

2. Rub chicken tenders with jerk seasoning. Skewer chicken and grill over medium-high heat until no longer pink, about 5 minutes per side.

3. Arrange lettuce and fruit on salad plates. Top with chicken and serve with dressing.

Makes 4 servings

Prep Time: 15 minutes
Cook Time: 10 minutes

Hula Chicken Salad with Orange Poppy Seed Dressing

Tropical Luau Cupcakes

- **2 cans (8 ounces each) crushed pineapple in juice**
- **1 package (18 1/4 ounces) yellow cake mix *without* pudding in the mix**
- **1 package (4-serving size) banana cream-flavor instant pudding and pie filling mix**
- **4 eggs**
- **1/3 cup vegetable oil**
- **1/4 teaspoon ground nutmeg**
- **1 container (12 ounces) whipped vanilla frosting**
- **3/4 cup flaked coconut, toasted**
- **3 to 4 medium kiwi**
- **30 (2 1/2-inch) pretzel sticks**

1. Preheat oven to 350°F. Line 30 standard (2 1/2-inch) muffin cups with paper baking cups. Drain pineapple, reserving juice. Set pineapple aside.

2. Beat reserved pineapple juice, cake mix, pudding mix, eggs, oil and nutmeg in large bowl with electric mixer at low speed 1 minute or until blended. Increase speed to medium; beat 1 to 2 minutes or until smooth. Fold in pineapple. Fill muffin cups two-thirds full.

3. Bake about 20 minutes or until toothpick inserted into centers comes out clean. Cool cupcakes in pans on wire rack 5 minutes; remove from pans and cool completely.

4. Frost tops of cupcakes with frosting; sprinkle with coconut. For palm trees,* peel kiwi and cut into 1/8-inch-thick slices. Create palm fronds by cutting each slice at 3/8-inch intervals, cutting from outside toward center. (Leave about 3/4- to 1-inch circle uncut in center of each slice). For palm tree trunk, push pretzel stick into, but not through, center of each kiwi slice. Push other end of pretzel into top of each cupcake. *Makes 30 cupcakes*

Palm tree decorations can be made up to 1 hour before serving.

Tip: To toast coconut, spread evenly on ungreased baking sheet; bake in preheated 350°F oven 4 to 6 minutes or until light golden brown, stirring frequently.

Tropical Luau Cupcakes

Hawaiian-Style Burgers

1 1/2 **pounds ground beef**
1/3 **cup chopped green onions**
2 **tablespoons Worcestershire sauce**
1/8 **teaspoon black pepper**
1/3 **cup pineapple preserves**
1/3 **cup barbecue sauce**
6 **pineapple slices**
6 **hamburger buns, split and toasted**

1. Combine beef, onions, Worcestershire and pepper in large bowl. Shape into six 1/2-inch-thick patties.

2. Combine preserves and barbecue sauce in small saucepan. Bring to a boil over medium heat, stirring often.

3. Spray grid with nonstick cooking spray. Prepare grill for direct cooking. Place patties on grid over medium coals. Grill, covered, 8 to 10 minutes (or, uncovered, 13 to 15 minutes) until cooked through (160°F), turning and brushing often with sauce. Place pineapple on grid; grill 1 minute or until browned, turning once.

4. Serve burgers on buns with pineapple.   *Makes 6 servings*

Broiling Directions: Arrange patties on rack in broiler pan. Broil 4 inches from heat until cooked through (160°F), turning and brushing often with sauce. Broil pineapple 1 minute, turning once.

Hawaiian-Style Burger

Patio Daddy-O

The fast-growing middle class was moving to suburbia

in record numbers. No backyard was complete without

a patio, a manicured lawn and the man of the house

cooking on the barbecue. Outdoor cookery was deemed

a manly occupation and steak was the he-man favorite.

Kabobs were a huge fad, too. Fifties specialties, such as

Surf & Turf Kabobs or Drunken T-Bone Steak, will feel

quite up-to-date in your own backyard today.

Mixed Grill Kabobs (page 148)

Peachy Smothered Pork Chops

- 1 tablespoon vegetable oil
- 1 small onion, finely minced
- 1 (12-ounce) jar peach preserves
- ⅔ cup *French's*® Honey Mustard
- 2 teaspoons grated peeled ginger root
- ¼ teaspoon ground nutmeg
- 6 boneless pork chops, cut 1-inch thick

1. Heat oil in small saucepan; sauté onion until tender. Stir in peach preserves, mustard, ginger and nutmeg. Heat to boiling; simmer 5 minutes until flavors are blended. Transfer ¾ cup sauce to bowl for basting. Reserve remaining sauce; keep warm.

2. Grill or broil chops over medium direct heat 20 minutes until barely pink in center, turning and basting often with sauce.

3. Serve chops with reserved sauce mixture.   *Makes 6 servings*

Alternate Method: For alternate skillet method, brown chops in skillet. Pour peach mixture over chops and simmer until no longer pink in center.

Prep Time: 5 minutes
Cook Time: 25 minutes

Peachy Smothered Pork Chop

Patio Daddy-O

Grilled T-Bone Steaks With BBQ Rub

2 to 4 well-trimmed beef **T-Bone** or **Porterhouse** steaks, cut 1 inch thick
(about 2 to 4 pounds)

BBQ RUB:
2 tablespoons chili powder
2 tablespoons packed brown sugar
1 tablespoon ground cumin
2 teaspoons minced garlic
2 teaspoons cider vinegar
1 teaspoon Worcestershire sauce
1/4 teaspoon ground red pepper

1. Combine rub ingredients; press evenly onto beef steaks.

2. Place steaks on grid over medium, ash-covered coals. Grill, uncovered,
14 to 16 minutes for medium rare to medium doneness, turning occasionally.
Remove bones and carve steaks into slices, if desired. Season with salt, as desired.

Makes 4 servings.

Tip: To broil, place steaks on rack in broiler pan so surface of beef is 3 to 4 inches
from heat. Broil 15 to 20 minutes for medium rare to medium doneness, turning once.

Prep and cook time: 25 minutes

Favorite recipe from **National Cattlemen's Beef Association on behalf of
The Beef Checkoff**

Grilled T-Bone Steaks With BBQ Rub

Blue Cheese Burgers with Red Onion

- **2** pounds ground beef chuck
- **2** cloves garlic, minced
- **1** teaspoon salt
- **$^1/_2$** teaspoon black pepper
- **4** ounces blue cheese
- **$^1/_3$** cup coarsely chopped walnuts, toasted
- **1** torpedo (long) red onion *or* **2** small red onions, sliced into $^3/_8$-inch-thick rounds
- **2** baguettes (each **1 2** inches long)
- Olive or vegetable oil

Combine beef, garlic, salt and pepper in medium bowl. Shape meat mixture into 12 oval patties. Mash cheese and blend with walnuts in small bowl. Divide cheese mixture equally; place on centers of 6 meat patties. Top with remaining meat patties; tightly pinch edges together to seal in filling.

Oil hot grid to help prevent sticking. Grill patties and onion, if desired, on covered grill, over medium KINGSFORD® Briquets, 7 to 12 minutes for medium doneness (160°F), turning once. Cut baguettes into 4-inch lengths; split each piece and brush cut side with olive oil. Move cooked burgers to edge of grill to keep warm. Grill bread, oil side down, until lightly toasted. Serve burgers on toasted baguettes.

Makes 6 servings

Blue Cheese Burger with Red Onion

Patio Daddy-O

Marinated Flank Steak with Pineapple

1 can (15 1/4 ounces) DEL MONTE® Sliced Pineapple In Its Own Juice
1/4 cup teriyaki sauce
2 tablespoons honey
1 pound beef flank steak

1. Drain pineapple, reserving 2 tablespoons juice. Set aside pineapple for later use.

2. Combine reserved juice, teriyaki sauce and honey in shallow 2-quart dish; mix well. Add meat; turn to coat. Cover and refrigerate at least 30 minutes or overnight.

3. Remove meat from marinade, reserving marinade. Grill meat over hot coals (or broil), brushing occasionally with reserved marinade. (Do not baste during last 5 minutes of cooking.) Cook about 4 minutes on each side for rare (140°F); about 5 minutes on each side for medium (160°F); or about 6 minutes on each side for well done (170°F). During last 4 minutes of cooking, grill pineapple until heated through.

4. Slice meat across grain; serve with pineapple. Garnish, if desired.

Makes 4 servings

Note: Marinade that has come into contact with raw meat must be discarded or boiled for several minutes before serving with cooked food.

Prep and Marinate Time: 35 minutes
Cook Time: 8 to 12 minutes

146

Marinated Flank Steak with Pineapple

Mixed Grill Kabobs

    1 pound boneless beef sirloin, cut into 1-inch cubes

    2 large red, orange or yellow bell peppers, cut into chunks

 12 strips bacon, blanched*

 12 ounces smoked sausage or kielbasa, cut into $1/2$-inch slices

    1 cup red pearl onions, peeled or red onion chunks

    1 pound pork tenderloin, cut lengthwise in half; then into $1/4$-inch wide long strips**

    1 cup pineapple wedges

 1 $1/2$ cups *Cattlemen's*® Award Winning Classic Barbecue Sauce

*To blanch bacon, place bacon strips into boiling water for 1 minute. Drain thoroughly.

**To easily cut pork, freeze about 30 minutes until very firm.

1. Arrange beef cubes and 1 bell pepper on metal skewers, weaving bacon strips around all. Place sausage, 1 pepper and onions on separate skewers. Ribbon strips of pork on additional skewers with pineapple wedges.

2. Baste the different kabobs with some of the barbecue sauce. Cook on a well-greased grill over medium-high direct heat, basting often with remaining barbecue sauce.

3. Serve a trio of kabobs to each person with additional sauce.

Makes 6 to 8 servings

Tip: You may substitute Cattlemen's® Authentic Smoke House or Golden Honey Barbecue Sauce.

Prep Time: 20 minutes
Cook Time: 10 to 15 minutes

Javanese Pork Saté

  1 pound boneless pork loin
  ½ cup minced onion
  2 tablespoons peanut butter
  2 tablespoons lemon juice
  2 tablespoons soy sauce
  1 tablespoon brown sugar
  1 tablespoon vegetable oil
  1 clove garlic, minced
    Dash hot pepper sauce

Cut pork into ½-inch cubes; place in shallow dish. In blender or food processor combine remaining ingredients. Blend until smooth. Pour over pork. Cover and marinate in refrigerator 10 minutes. Thread pork onto skewers. (If using bamboo skewers, soak in water 1 hour to prevent burning.)

Grill or broil 10 to 12 minutes, turning occasionally, until done. Serve with hot cooked rice, if desired.

Makes 4 servings

Favorite recipe from **National Pork Board**

helpful hint:

Saté (or satay) is meat that is marinated, skewered and grilled, similar to a kabob. Saté is often served with a peanut or soy-based dipping sauce. In some Asian countries, it is a popular snack sold by street vendors.

Espresso-Bourbon Steaks with Mashed Sweet Potatoes

4 beef tenderloin steaks, cut 1 inch thick (about 4 ounces each)
2 to 4 teaspoons coarsely cracked black pepper
Mashed Sweet Potatoes (recipe follows)
Steamed green beans

ESPRESSO-BOURBON SAUCE:
$^1/_4$ cup bourbon
$^1/_4$ cup maple syrup
$^1/_4$ cup reduced sodium soy sauce
1 tablespoon fresh lemon juice
2 teaspoons instant espresso coffee powder
$^1/_8$ teaspoon black pepper

1. Combine all sauce ingredients, except pepper, in small saucepan; bring to a boil. Reduce heat and simmer, uncovered 12 to 15 minutes or until sauce is thickened and reduced by about half, stirring occasionally. Stir in pepper. Keep warm.

2. Prepare Mashed Sweet Potatoes. Meanwhile press coarsely cracked pepper on both sides of beef steak. Place steaks on grid over medium, ash-covered coals. Grill, uncovered, 13 to 15 minutes for medium rare doneness, turning once.

3. Evenly divide sauce onto 4 plates. Place steak on top of sauce. Serve with Mashed Sweet Potatoes and green beans.   *Makes 4 servings.*

Mashed Sweet Potatoes: Place 9 ounces peeled and cubed sweet potatoes and 1 teaspoon salt in large saucepan. Cover with water; bring to a boil. Cook 4 to 5 minutes or until potatoes are tender. Drain. Combine potatoes, 2 tablespoons butter, $^1/_8$ teaspoon salt and $^1/_8$ teaspoon black pepper. Beat until mashed and smooth.

Prep and cook time: 45 minutes

Favorite recipe from **National Cattlemen's Beef Association on behalf of The Beef Checkoff**

Espresso-Bourbon Steak with Mashed Sweet Potatoes

Carolina-Style Barbecue Chicken

2 pounds boneless skinless chicken breast halves or thighs
³/₄ cup packed light brown sugar, divided
³/₄ cup *French's® Classic Yellow®* Mustard
¹/₂ cup cider vinegar
¹/₄ cup *Frank's® RedHot®* Original Cayenne Pepper Sauce
2 tablespoons vegetable oil
2 tablespoons *French's®* Worcestershire Sauce
¹/₂ teaspoon salt
¹/₄ teaspoon black pepper

1. Place chicken in large resealable plastic food storage bag. Combine ¹/₂ cup brown sugar, mustard, vinegar, *Frank's RedHot* Sauce, oil, Worcestershire, salt and pepper in 4-cup measure; mix well. Pour 1 cup mustard mixture over chicken. Seal bag; marinate in refrigerator 1 hour or overnight.

2. Pour remaining mustard mixture into small saucepan. Stir in remaining ¹/₄ cup brown sugar. Bring to a boil. Reduce heat; simmer 5 minutes or until sugar dissolves and mixture thickens slightly, stirring often. Reserve for serving sauce.

3. Place chicken on well-oiled grid, reserving marinade. Grill over high heat 10 to 15 minutes or until chicken is no longer pink in center, turning and basting once with marinade. *Do not baste during last 5 minutes of cooking.* Discard any remaining marinade. Serve chicken with reserved sauce. *Makes 8 servings*

Prep Time: 15 minutes
Marinate Time: 1 hour
Cook Time: 10 minutes

Carolina-Style Barbecue Chicken

Cavemen Beef Back Ribs

$^{1}/_{4}$ **cup paprika**

$^{1}/_{4}$ **cup brown sugar**

$^{1}/_{4}$ **cup seasoned salt**

  2 full racks beef back ribs, split in half (about 6 to 8 pounds)

  1 cup *Cattlemen's*® Authentic Smoke House Barbecue Sauce

$^{1}/_{4}$ **cup apple, pineapple or orange juice**

1. Combine paprika, sugar and seasoned salt. Rub mixture into ribs. Cover ribs and refrigerate 1 to 3 hours.

2. Prepare grill for indirect cooking over medium-low heat (250°F). Place ribs on rib rack or in foil pan. Cook on covered grill 2$^{1}/_{2}$ to 3 hours until very tender.

3. Meanwhile, combine barbecue sauce and juice. Brush mixture on ribs during last 30 minutes of cooking. Serve with additional barbecue sauce.

Makes 6 to 8 servings

Tip: For very tender ribs, remove membrane from underside of ribs before cooking. With a sharp paring knife, score membrane on bone from underside of ribs. Lift up portions of membrane with point of knife. Using kitchen towel, pull membrane away from bone and discard.

Prep Time: 5 minutes
Cook Time: 3 hours
Marinate Time: 1 hour

Cavemen Beef Back Ribs

The All-American Burger

Burger Spread (recipe follows)
1 ½ **pounds ground beef**
  2 **tablespoons chopped fresh parsley**
  2 **teaspoons onion powder**
  2 **teaspoons Worcestershire sauce**
  1 **teaspoon garlic powder**
  1 **teaspoon salt**
  1 **teaspoon black pepper**
  4 **hamburger buns, split**

1. Prepare Burger Spread; set aside.

2. Prepare grill for direct cooking.

3. Combine beef, parsley, onion powder, Worcestershire sauce, garlic powder, salt and pepper in medium bowl; mix lightly but thoroughly. Shape mixture into four ½-inch-thick burgers.

4. Place burgers on grid. Grill, covered, over medium heat 8 to 10 minutes (or, uncovered, 13 to 15 minutes) to medium (160°F) or to desired doneness, turning halfway through grilling time.

5. Remove burgers from grill. Serve burgers on buns with Burger Spread.

Makes 4 servings

Burger Spread

- ¹/₂ cup ketchup
- ¹/₄ cup prepared mustard
- 2 tablespoons chopped onion
- 1 tablespoon relish or chopped pickles
- 1 tablespoon chopped fresh parsley

Combine all ingredients in small bowl; mix well.　　　　　　*Makes 1 cup*

Serving Suggestion: Accompany burger with fries, chips, garden salad, coleslaw or potato salad.

Grilled Sherry Pork Chops

- ¹/₄ cup HOLLAND HOUSE® Sherry Cooking Wine
- ¹/₄ cup GRANDMA'S® Molasses
- 2 tablespoons soy sauce
- 4 pork chops (1 inch thick)

In plastic bowl, combine sherry, molasses and soy sauce; pour over pork chops. Cover; refrigerate 30 minutes. Prepare grill. Drain pork chops, reserving marinade. Grill pork chops over medium-high heat 20 to 30 minutes or until pork is no longer pink in center, turning once and brushing frequently with reserved marinade.* Discard any remaining marinade.　　　　　　*Makes 4 servings*

Do not baste during last 5 minutes of grilling.

Drunken T-Bone Steak

2 T-bone steaks, cut 1-inch thick (about 3 pounds)
1 cup *French's*® Worcestershire Sauce
½ cup *Cattlemen's*® Authentic Smoke House Barbecue Sauce
3 tablespoons bourbon
2 tablespoons butter
2 tablespoons *French's*® Worcestershire Sauce
4 teaspoons garlic and pepper steak seasoning

1. Place steaks into resealable plastic food storage bag. Pour 1 cup Worcestershire over steaks. Marinate in refrigerator 1 to 3 hours.

2. Meanwhile, prepare sauce. Combine barbecue sauce, bourbon, butter and 2 tablespoons Worcestershire in saucepan. Heat to boiling. Simmer 3 minutes; reserve.

3. Drain steaks. Rub steak seasoning into meat, coating both sides. Cook steaks over high direct heat, about 7 minutes per side for medium-rare (145°F) or to desired doneness. Let steaks rest 10 minutes before slicing. Serve with sauce on the side.

Makes 4 servings

Prep Time: 5 minutes
Cook Time: 15 minutes
Marinate Time: 1 hour

Drunken T-Bone Steak

159

Herb Orange Pork Chops

1 ½ cups orange juice

  4 tablespoons vegetable oil, divided

1 ½ teaspoons salt

1 ½ teaspoons freshly ground black pepper

  2 cloves garlic, crushed

  1 teaspoon dried thyme

  4 pork loin chops, cut ¾ inch thick

  ½ cup thinly sliced green onions

  1 teaspoon grated orange peel

1. Combine orange juice, 3 tablespoons oil, salt, pepper, garlic and thyme in small bowl. Place chops and ¾ cup marinade in large resealable food storage bag; seal bag. Marinate in refrigerator at least 1 hour. Reserve remaining 1 cup marinade.

2. Remove chops from marinade; discard bag and marinade. Grill or broil chops 10 to 15 minutes or until barely pink in center, turning halfway through grilling time.

3. Meanwhile, heat remaining 1 tablespoon oil in large skillet. Add onions and orange peel; cook over medium heat 1 minute. Stir in reserved marinade. Reduce heat to low; cook until reduced by half. Serve over chops.

Makes 4 servings

Herb Orange Pork Chop

Patio Daddy-O

Surf & Turf Kabobs

  1 pound beef tenderloin, cut into 1 1/4-inch chunks
12 jumbo or colossal raw shrimp, peeled and deveined, tails on
  1 medium onion, cut into 12 wedges
  1 red or yellow bell pepper, cut into 1-inch chunks
1/3 cup unsalted butter
  3 tablespoons lemon juice
  3 cloves garlic, minced
  2 teaspoons paprika or smoked paprika
  1 teaspoon salt
1/4 teaspoon black pepper or ground red pepper
   Lemon wedges

1. Prepare grill for direct cooking. Alternately thread beef, shrimp, onion and bell pepper onto 12-inch-long metal skewers. (Skewer shrimp through ends to form "C" shape for even cooking.)

2. Melt butter in small saucepan. Stir in lemon juice, garlic, paprika, salt and black pepper.

3. Place skewers on grid over medium coals; brush with half of butter sauce. Grill 5 minutes; turn and brush with remaining butter sauce. Continue grilling 5 to 6 minutes or until shrimp are opaque (beef will be medium-rare to medium doneness). Serve with lemon wedges. *Makes 4 servings*

Surf & Turf Kabobs

163

Patio Daddy-O

Garlic & Lemon Herb Marinated Chicken

3 to 4 pounds bone-in chicken pieces, skinned if desired
1/3 cup *French's®* Honey Dijon Mustard
1/3 cup lemon juice
1/3 cup olive oil
3 cloves garlic, minced
1 tablespoon grated lemon zest
1 tablespoon minced fresh thyme or rosemary
1 teaspoon coarse salt
1/2 teaspoon coarse black pepper

1. Place chicken into resealable plastic food storage bag. Combine remaining ingredients. Pour over chicken. Marinate in refrigerator 1 to 3 hours.

2. Remove chicken from marinade. Grill chicken over medium direct heat for 35 to 45 minutes until juices run clear near bone (170°F for breast meat; 180°F for dark meat). Serve with additional mustard on the side.   *Makes 4 servings*

Tip: This marinade is also great on whole chicken or pork chops.

Prep Time: 10 minutes
Cook Time: 45 minutes
Marinate Time: 1 hour

Garlic & Lemon Herb Marinated Chicken

Cool Cat Cakes

Creating a cake became a lot easier with modern conveniences like electric mixers and cake mixes. Now homemakers could produce lofty layer cakes and fluffy frosting without slaving for hours in the kitchen. Classic cakes, including Lady Baltimore Cake and Hershey's Red Velvet Cake, were the perfect centerpiece for a celebration in the '50s and still are today. With these recipes, it's easy to bake some memories.

German Chocolate Cake (page 176)

Carmen Miranda Cake

1 1/3 cups cake flour
3/4 teaspoon baking powder
1/4 teaspoon salt
3/4 cup (1 1/2 sticks) unsalted butter, softened
2/3 cup granulated sugar
3 eggs
1/2 cup vanilla low-fat yogurt
1 teaspoon vanilla
3/4 cup (6 ounces) frozen tropical fruit punch concentrate
2 tablespoons honey
1 tablespoon dark rum
2 teaspoons cornstarch
2 cups fruit chunks (pineapple, peach, star fruit, kiwi, watermelon, berries, grapes)

1. Preheat oven to 350°F. Grease and flour 8×4-inch loaf pan. Sift together flour, baking powder and salt in medium bowl.

2. Beat butter and sugar in large bowl with electric mixer until fluffy. Beat in eggs one at a time. Beat in yogurt and vanilla. Gradually add flour mixture and beat until blended. Scrape down side of bowl as necessary. Spread batter in prepared pan.

3. Bake 50 to 60 minutes or until toothpick inserted into center comes out clean; cool 20 minutes. Turn out onto wire rack to cool completely.

4. Meanwhile, prepare glaze. Combine fruit punch concentrate and honey in small saucepan. Bring to a boil over medium heat, stirring to dissolve honey. Boil 5 minutes. Mix rum and cornstarch together in small bowl; stir into hot fruit mixture and cook 1 minute or until thickened. Let glaze cool to room temperature.

5. Set cake on wire rack over baking sheet. Brush thick coat of glaze over cake top, allowing some to flow down sides. Arrange fruit chunks on top. Pour remaining glaze over fruit and cake top. Let stand at room temperature at least 1 hour before serving.

Makes 8 servings

Carmen Miranda Cake

Fudge Ribbon Cake

1 (18.25- or 18.5-ounce) package chocolate cake mix
1 (8-ounce) package cream cheese, softened
2 tablespoons butter or margarine, softened
1 tablespoon cornstarch
1 (14-ounce) can **EAGLE BRAND**® Sweetened Condensed Milk (**NOT** evaporated milk)
1 egg
1 teaspoon vanilla extract
Chocolate Glaze (recipe follows)

1. Preheat oven to 350°F. Grease and flour 13×9-inch baking pan. Prepare cake mix as package directs. Pour batter into prepared pan.

2. In small bowl, beat cream cheese, butter and cornstarch until fluffy. Gradually beat in EAGLE BRAND®. Add egg and vanilla; beat until smooth. Spoon evenly over cake batter.

3. Bake 40 minutes or until toothpick inserted near center comes out clean. Cool. Drizzle with chocolate glaze. Store leftovers covered in refrigerator.

Makes 10 to 12 servings

Chocolate Glaze: In small saucepan, over low heat, melt 1 (1-ounce) square unsweetened or semisweet chocolate and 1 tablespoon butter or margarine with 2 tablespoons water. Remove from heat. Stir in ¾ cup confectioners' sugar and ½ teaspoon vanilla extract. Stir until smooth and well blended. Makes about ⅓ cup glaze.

Fudge Ribbon Bundt Cake: Preheat oven to 350°F. Grease and flour 10-inch Bundt pan. Prepare cake mix as package directs. Pour batter into prepared pan. Prepare cream cheese layer as directed above; spoon evenly over batter. Bake 50 to 55 minutes or until toothpick inserted near center comes out clean. Cool 10 minutes. Remove from pan. Cool. Prepare Chocolate Glaze and drizzle over cake. Store leftovers covered in refrigerator.

Fudge Ribbon Cake

Cool Cat Cakes

Pretty-in-Pink Peppermint Cupcakes

1 package (18¼ ounces) white cake mix
1⅓ cups water
3 egg whites
2 tablespoons vegetable oil or melted butter
½ teaspoon peppermint extract
3 to 4 drops red liquid food coloring *or* ¼ teaspoon gel food coloring
1 container (16 ounces) prepared vanilla frosting
½ cup crushed peppermint candies (about 16 candies)

1. Preheat oven to 350°F. Line 30 standard (2½-inch) muffin cups with pink or white paper baking cups.

2. Beat cake mix, water, egg whites, oil, peppermint extract and food coloring in large bowl with electric mixer at low speed 30 seconds. Beat at medium speed 2 minutes.

3. Spoon batter into prepared muffin cups, filling three-fourths full. Bake 20 to 22 minutes or until toothpick inserted into centers comes out clean. Cool in pans on wire racks 10 minutes. Remove cupcakes to racks; cool completely. (At this point, cupcakes may be frozen up to 3 months. Thaw at room temperature before frosting.)

4. Spread frosting over cooled cupcakes; sprinkle with crushed candies. Store at room temperature up to 24 hours or cover and refrigerate up to 3 days before serving.

Makes 30 cupcakes

helpful hint:

This recipe can be easily adapted for your favorite flavors. Try substituting almond extract for the peppermint and topping with chocolate-covered almonds.

Pretty-in-Pink Peppermint Cupcakes

Pumpkin Pecan Rum Cake

³/₄ cup chopped pecans
3 cups all-purpose flour
2 tablespoons pumpkin pie spice
2 teaspoons baking soda
1 teaspoon salt
1 cup (2 sticks) butter or margarine, softened
1 cup packed brown sugar
1 cup granulated sugar
4 large eggs
1 can (15 ounces) LIBBY'S® 100% Pure Pumpkin
1 teaspoon vanilla extract
   Rum Butter Glaze (recipe follows)

PREHEAT oven to 325°F. Grease 12-cup Bundt pan. Sprinkle nuts over bottom.

COMBINE flour, pumpkin pie spice, baking soda and salt in medium bowl. Beat butter, brown sugar and granulated sugar in large mixer bowl until light and fluffy. Add eggs; beat well. Add pumpkin and vanilla extract; beat well. Add flour mixture to pumpkin mixture, ¹/₃ at a time, mixing well after each addition. Spoon batter into prepared pan.

BAKE for 60 to 70 minutes or until wooden pick comes out clean. Cool 10 minutes. Make holes in cake with long pick; pour *half* of glaze over cake. Let stand 5 minutes and invert onto plate. Make holes in top of cake; pour *remaining* glaze over cake. Cool. Garnish as desired.   *Makes 24 servings*

Rum Butter Glaze: **MELT** ¹/₄ cup butter or margarine in small saucepan; stir in ¹/₂ cup granulated sugar and 2 tablespoons water. Bring to a boil. Remove from heat; stir in 2 to 3 tablespoons dark rum or 1 teaspoon rum extract.

Pumpkin Pecan Rum Cake

German Chocolate Cake

¼ cup **HERSHEY'S Cocoa**
½ cup boiling water
1 cup (2 sticks) plus 3 tablespoons butter or margarine, softened
2¼ cups sugar
1 teaspoon vanilla extract
4 eggs
2 cups all-purpose flour
1 teaspoon baking soda
½ teaspoon salt
1 cup buttermilk or sour milk*
Coconut Pecan Frosting (recipe follows)
Pecan halves (optional)

*To sour milk: Use 1 tablespoon white vinegar plus milk to equal 1 cup.

1. Heat oven to 350°F. Grease and flour three 9-inch round baking pans. Combine cocoa and water in small bowl; stir until smooth. Set aside to cool.

2. Beat butter, sugar and vanilla in large bowl until fluffy. Add eggs, one at a time, beating well after each addition. Stir together flour, baking soda and salt; add alternately with chocolate mixture and buttermilk to butter mixture. Mix only until smooth. Pour batter into prepared pans.

3. Bake 25 to 30 minutes or until top springs back when touched lightly. Cool 5 minutes; remove from pans. Cool completely on wire rack. Prepare Coconut Pecan Frosting; spread between layers and over top. Garnish with pecan halves, if desired.

Makes 10 to 12 servings

Coconut Pecan Frosting

  1 can (14 ounces) sweetened condensed milk (not evaporated milk)
  3 egg yolks, slightly beaten
  $^1\!/_2$ cup (1 stick) butter or margarine
  1 teaspoon vanilla extract
 1 $^1\!/_3$ cups MOUNDS® Sweetened Coconut Flakes
  1 cup chopped pecans

1. Place sweetened condensed milk, egg yolks and butter in medium saucepan. Cook over low heat, stirring constantly, until mixture is thickened and bubbly.

2. Remove from heat; stir in vanilla, coconut and pecans. Cool to room temperature.

Makes about 2$^2\!/_3$ cups frosting

Grandma's® Gingerbread

 $^1\!/_2$ cup shortening or butter
 $^1\!/_2$ cup sugar
 1 cup GRANDMA'S® Molasses
 2 eggs
2 $^1\!/_2$ cups all-purpose flour
 2 teaspoons baking powder
 2 teaspoons cinnamon
 1 teaspoon salt
 1 teaspoon ground ginger
 $^1\!/_2$ teaspoon baking soda
 $^1\!/_2$ teaspoon ground cloves
 1 cup hot water

Heat oven to 350°F. In medium bowl, blend shortening with sugar. Add molasses and eggs; beat well. Sift dry ingredients; add alternately with water to molasses mixture. Bake in greased 9-inch square pan about 50 minutes. *Makes 8 servings*

Chocolate Chiffon Cake

- 1 cup all-purpose flour
- 1 teaspoon baking powder
- $^{1}/_{2}$ teaspoon salt
- 4 (1-ounce) squares semisweet chocolate
- $^{1}/_{2}$ cup hot water
- 5 eggs, separated
- $^{2}/_{3}$ cup granulated sugar
- 1 teaspoon vanilla
- Powdered sugar

1. Preheat oven to 350°F. Combine flour, baking powder and salt in small bowl; set aside.

2. Combine chocolate and hot water in small heavy saucepan. Melt chocolate over low heat, stirring occasionally; set aside.

3. Beat egg whites in clean large bowl with electric mixer at high speed until foamy. Gradually beat in sugar until stiff peaks form; set aside.

4. Combine melted chocolate mixture, egg yolks and vanilla in large bowl. Beat with electric mixer at low speed until well blended. Gradually add flour mixture to chocolate mixture. Beat with electric mixer at low speed until well blended.

5. Gently fold chocolate mixture into egg white mixture with rubber spatula until chocolate mixture is evenly incorporated into egg white mixture.

6. Pour into *ungreased* 10-inch tube pan. Run spatula through batter to break up any large air bubbles. Bake 45 to 50 minutes or until top springs back when lightly touched.

7. Invert cake in pan onto metal funnel or bottle. Cool completely. Remove from pan.

Makes about 12 servings

Chocolate Chiffon Cake

179

Pineapple Upside-Down Cake

TOPPING

  1/2 cup (1 stick) butter or margarine
  1 cup firmly packed brown sugar
  1 can (20 ounces) pineapple slices, well drained
  Maraschino cherries, drained and halved
  Walnut halves

CAKE

  1 package **DUNCAN HINES**® Moist Deluxe® Pineapple Supreme Cake Mix
  1 package (4-serving size) vanilla-flavor instant pudding and pie filling mix
  4 eggs
  1 cup water
  1/2 cup oil

1. Preheat oven to 350°F.

2. For topping, melt butter over low heat in 12-inch cast-iron skillet or skillet with ovenproof handle. Remove from heat. Stir in brown sugar. Spread to cover bottom of skillet. Arrange pineapple slices, maraschino cherries and walnut halves in skillet. Set aside.

3. For cake, combine cake mix, pudding mix, eggs, water and oil in large mixing bowl. Beat at medium speed with electric mixer for 2 minutes. Pour batter evenly over fruit in skillet. Bake at 350°F for 1 hour or until toothpick inserted in center comes out clean. Invert onto serving plate. *Makes 16 to 20 servings*

Tip: Cake can be made in a 13×9×2-inch pan. Bake at 350°F for 45 to 55 minutes or until toothpick inserted in center comes out clean. Cake is also delicious using Duncan Hines® Moist Deluxe® Yellow Cake Mix.

Pineapple Upside-Down Cake

Cool Cat Cakes

Mini Neapolitan Ice Cream Cakes

1 package (18 ¼ ounces) vanilla cake mix
¾ cup water
3 eggs
⅓ cup vegetable oil
⅓ cup unsweetened cocoa powder
4 cups slightly softened strawberry ice cream
Powdered sugar, dark chocolate curls and strawberry fans (optional)

1. Preheat oven to 350°F. Spray 4 (5×3-inch) mini loaf pans with nonstick cooking spray.

2. Combine cake mix, water, eggs and oil in large bowl. Beat with electric mixer at low speed 30 seconds or until just blended. Beat 2 minutes at medium speed or until well blended. Reserve 1¾ cups batter. Add cocoa to remaining batter; stir until well blended.

3. Divide chocolate batter evenly between 2 prepared pans. Divide reserved plain batter evenly between remaining 2 prepared pans.

4. Bake 30 minutes or until toothpicks inserted into centers come out clean. Cool in pans 10 minutes. Remove cakes from pans to wire racks; cool completely.

5. Trim rounded tops of cakes with serrated knife; discard trimmings. Cut each cake in half horizontally. Line 4 clean mini loaf pans with plastic wrap, leaving 2-inch overhang on all sides. Place 1 vanilla cake layer in each pan.

6. Place ice cream in large bowl; beat with electric mixer at medium speed about 30 seconds or just until spreadable. Spread 1 cup ice cream over each vanilla cake layer in pans; top with chocolate cake layers. Cover with plastic wrap; freeze at least 4 hours.

7. Remove cakes from pans; trim any uneven sides. Garnish with powdered sugar, dark chocolate curls and strawberry fans. To serve, cut each cake into 3 slices.

Makes 4 cakes (12 servings)

Mini Neapolitan Ice Cream Cakes

Lady Baltimore Cake

3 1/4 cups all-purpose flour
4 1/2 teaspoons baking powder
1 1/2 teaspoons salt
2 1/4 cups sugar
1 1/4 cups shortening
   2 teaspoons vanilla
1 1/2 cups milk
   8 egg whites, at room temperature
     Filling (recipe follows)
     Frosting (recipe follows)

1. Preheat oven to 350°F. Grease 3 (9-inch) round cake pans. Line bottom of pans with waxed paper. Sift together flour, baking powder and salt in medium bowl.

2. Beat sugar and shortening in large bowl until light and fluffy. Blend in vanilla. Add dry ingredients alternately with milk, beating well after each addition.

3. Beat egg whites in another large bowl with electric mixer at high speed until stiff peaks form; fold into batter. Pour evenly into prepared pans.

4. Bake 30 minutes or until toothpick inserted into centers comes out clean. Cool layers in pans on wire racks 10 minutes. Loosen edges and remove to racks to cool completely. Prepare Filling and Frosting.

5. To assemble, spread two cake layers with Filling; stack on cake plate. Top with remaining cake layer. Frost with Frosting.   *Makes one 3-layer cake*

Filling

  ½ cup (1 stick) butter
  1 cup sugar
  ½ cup water
  ⅓ cup bourbon or brandy
  10 egg yolks, lightly beaten
  1 cup finely chopped raisins
  ¾ cup chopped pecans
  ½ cup flaked coconut
  ½ cup chopped drained maraschino cherries
  ¾ teaspoon vanilla

1. Melt butter in 2-quart saucepan. Stir in sugar, water and bourbon. Bring to a boil over medium-high heat, stirring occasionally to dissolve sugar. Stir small amount of hot mixture into egg yolks. Add egg yolk mixture to remaining hot mixture in saucepan. Cook and stir until thickened; remove from heat.

2. Stir in raisins, pecans, coconut and cherries. Blend in vanilla. Cool completely.

Frosting

  1½ cups sugar
  ½ cup water
  2 egg whites*
  2 teaspoons corn syrup or ¼ teaspoon cream of tartar
  Dash salt
  1 teaspoon vanilla

*Use clean, uncracked eggs.

Combine sugar, water, egg whites, corn syrup and salt in top of double boiler. Beat with electric mixer at medium speed over simmering water 7 minutes or until mixture stands in soft peaks. Remove from heat; add vanilla. Beat until frosting is of spreading consistency.

Chocolate Orange Marble Chiffon Cake

$^1/_3$ cup **HERSHEY'S** Cocoa

$^1/_4$ cup hot water

3 tablespoons plus 1 $^1/_2$ cups sugar, divided

2 tablespoons plus $^1/_2$ cup vegetable oil, divided

2 $^1/_4$ cups all-purpose flour

1 tablespoon baking powder

1 teaspoon salt

$^3/_4$ cup cold water

7 egg yolks

1 cup egg whites (about 8)

$^1/_2$ teaspoon cream of tartar

1 tablespoon freshly grated orange peel

Orange Glaze (page 188)

1. Remove top oven rack; move other rack to lowest position. Heat oven to 325°F.

2. Stir together cocoa and hot water in medium bowl. Stir in 3 tablespoons sugar and 2 tablespoons oil; set aside. Stir together flour, remaining 1 $^1/_2$ cups sugar, baking powder and salt in large bowl. Add cold water, remaining $^1/_2$ cup oil and egg yolks; beat with spoon until smooth.

3. Beat egg whites and cream of tartar in another large bowl on high speed of mixer until stiff peaks form. Pour egg yolk mixture in a thin stream over egg white mixture, gently folding just until blended. Remove 2 cups batter; add to chocolate mixture, gently folding until well blended. Fold orange peel into remaining batter.

4. Spoon half the orange batter into ungreased 10-inch tube pan; drop half the chocolate batter on top by spoonfuls. Repeat layers of orange and chocolate batters. Gently swirl with knife for marbled effect.

5. Bake 1 hour and 15 to 20 minutes or until top springs back when lightly touched. Immediately invert cake onto heatproof funnel; cool cake completely. Remove cake from pan; invert onto serving plate. Prepare Orange Glaze; spread over top of cake.

Makes 12 to 16 servings

186

continued on page 188

Chocolate Orange Marble Chiffon Cake

Cool Cat Cakes

Chocolate Orange Marble Chiffon Cake, continued

Orange Glaze

¹/₃ **cup butter or margarine**
 2 **cups powdered sugar**
 2 **tablespoons orange juice**
¹/₂ **teaspoon freshly grated orange peel**

Melt butter in medium saucepan over low heat. Remove from heat; gradually stir in powdered sugar, orange juice and orange peel, beating until smooth and of desired consistency. Add additional orange juice, 1 teaspoon at a time if needed.

Makes 1 cup glaze

Blueberry Angel Food Cake Rolls

 1 **package DUNCAN HINES® Angel Food Cake Mix**
¹/₄ **cup confectioners' sugar plus additional for dusting towels**
 1 **can (21 ounces) blueberry pie filling**
 Mint leaves for garnish (optional)

1. Preheat oven to 350°F. Line two 15¹/₂×10¹/₂×1-inch jelly-roll pans with aluminum foil.

2. Prepare cake mix as directed on package. Divide and spread evenly into prepared pans. Cut through batter with knife or spatula to remove large air bubbles. Bake at 350°F for 15 minutes or until set. Invert cakes at once onto clean, lint-free dishtowels dusted with confectioners' sugar. Remove foil carefully. Roll up each cake with towel jelly-roll fashion, starting at short end. Cool completely.

3. Unroll cakes. Spread about 1 cup blueberry pie filling to within 1 inch of edges on each cake. Reroll and place seam-side down on serving plate. Dust with ¹/₄ cup confectioners' sugar. Garnish with mint leaves, if desired

Makes 2 cakes (8 servings each)

Blueberry Angel Food Cake Roll

189

Cool Cat Cakes

Hershey's Red Velvet Cake

1/2 cup (1 stick) butter or margarine, softened
1 1/2 cups sugar
2 eggs
1 teaspoon vanilla extract
1 cup buttermilk or sour milk*
2 tablespoons (1-ounce bottle) red food color
2 cups all-purpose flour
1/3 cup HERSHEY'S Cocoa
1 teaspoon salt
1 1/2 teaspoons baking soda
1 tablespoon white vinegar
1 can (16 ounces) ready-to-spread vanilla frosting
    HERSHEY'S MINI CHIPS™ Semi-Sweet Chocolate Chips or HERSHEY'S Milk
    Chocolate Chips (optional)

*To sour milk: Use 1 tablespoon white vinegar plus milk to equal 1 cup.

1. Heat oven to 350°F. Grease and flour 13×9×2-inch baking pan.**

2. Beat butter and sugar in large bowl; add eggs and vanilla, beating well. Stir together buttermilk and food color. Stir together flour, cocoa and salt; add alternately to butter mixture with buttermilk mixture, mixing well. Stir in baking soda and vinegar. Pour into prepared pan.

3. Bake 30 to 35 minutes or until wooden pick inserted in center comes out clean. Cool completely in pan on wire rack. Frost; garnish with chocolate chips, if desired.

Makes about 15 servings

**This recipe can be made in 2 (9-inch) cake pans. Bake at 350°F for 30 to 35 minutes.*

Hershey's Red Velvet Cake

Strawberry Stripe Refrigerator Cake

CAKE
- 1 package **DUNCAN HINES®** Moist Deluxe® Classic White Cake Mix
- 2 packages (10 ounces) frozen sweetened strawberry slices, thawed

TOPPING
- 1 package (4-serving size) vanilla-flavor instant pudding and pie filling mix
- 1 cup milk
- 1 cup whipping cream, whipped
- Fresh strawberries for garnish (optional)

1. Preheat oven to 350°F. Grease and flour 13×9×2-inch pan.

2. For cake, prepare, bake and cool following package directions. Poke holes 1 inch apart in top of cake using handle of wooden spoon. Purée thawed strawberries with juice in blender or food processor. Spoon evenly over top of cake, allowing mixture to soak into holes.

3. For topping, combine pudding mix and milk in large bowl. Stir until smooth. Fold in whipped cream. Spread over cake. Decorate with fresh strawberries, if desired. Refrigerate at least 4 hours. *Makes 12 to 16 servings*

Variation: For a Neapolitan Refrigerator Cake, substitute Duncan Hines® Moist Deluxe® Devil's Food Cake Mix for White Cake Mix and follow directions listed above.

Strawberry Stripe Refrigerator Cake

Kookie Cookies

Cookies never go out of fashion. In the '50s, chocolate chips and "M&Ms"® joined the array of other favorite ingredients. Although cookies have been around in one form or another since ancient times, brownies are a more recent invention. Folklore claims they were created by a careless cook who forgot to put baking powder in her chocolate cake. Then or now, it's still true that a happy home is one with a filled cookie jar.

Original Nestlé® Toll House® Chocolate Chip Cookies (page 205)

Luscious Lemon Bars

2 cups all-purpose flour
1 cup **(2 sticks)** butter
$^1/_2$ cup powdered sugar
1 tablespoon plus **1** teaspoon grated lemon peel, divided
$^1/_4$ teaspoon salt
1 cup granulated sugar
3 eggs
$^1/_3$ cup fresh lemon juice
Sifted powdered sugar

1. Preheat oven to 350°F. Grease 13×9-inch baking pan; set aside.

2. Place flour, butter, $^1/_2$ cup powdered sugar, 1 teaspoon lemon peel and salt in food processor. Cover; process until mixture forms coarse crumbs. Press mixture evenly into prepared baking pan. Bake 18 to 20 minutes or until golden brown.

3. Beat granulated sugar, eggs, lemon juice and remaining 1 tablespoon lemon peel in medium bowl with electric mixer at medium speed until well blended.

4. Pour mixture evenly over warm crust. Return to oven; bake 18 to 20 minutes or until center is set and edges are golden brown. Remove pan to wire rack; cool completely.

5. Dust with sifted powdered sugar; cut into 2×1$^1/_2$-inch bars. Store tightly covered at room temperature. *Do not freeze.*   *Makes 3 dozen bars*

Luscious Lemon Bars

Kookie Cookies

Gingersnaps

2 ½ cups all-purpose flour
1 ½ teaspoons ground ginger
1 teaspoon baking soda
1 teaspoon ground allspice
½ teaspoon salt
1 ½ cups sugar
2 tablespoons margarine, softened
½ cup MOTT'S® Apple Sauce
¼ cup GRANDMA'S® Molasses

1. Preheat oven to 375°F. Spray cookie sheets with nonstick cooking spray.

2. In medium bowl, sift together flour, ginger, baking soda, allspice and salt.

3. In large bowl, beat sugar and margarine with electric mixer at medium speed until blended. Whisk in apple sauce and molasses.

4. Add flour mixture to apple sauce mixture; stir until well blended.

5. Drop rounded tablespoonfuls of dough 1 inch apart onto prepared cookie sheets. Flatten each slightly with moistened fingertips.

6. Bake 12 to 15 minutes or until firm. Cool completely on wire rack.

Makes 3 dozen cookies

Gingersnaps

Fudge Topped Brownies

    2 cups sugar
    1 cup (2 sticks) butter or margarine, melted
    1 cup all-purpose flour
    2/3 cup unsweetened cocoa
    1/2 teaspoon baking powder
    2 eggs
    1/2 cup milk
    3 teaspoons vanilla extract, divided
    1 cup chopped nuts (optional)
    2 cups (12 ounces) semisweet chocolate chips
    1 (14-ounce) can EAGLE BRAND® Sweetened Condensed Milk (NOT evaporated
        milk)
        Dash salt

1. Preheat oven to 350°F. In large bowl, combine sugar, butter, flour, cocoa, baking powder, eggs, milk and 1 1/2 teaspoons vanilla; mix well. Stir in nuts (optional). Spread in greased 13×9-inch baking pan. Bake 40 minutes or until brownies begin to pull away from sides of pan.

2. In heavy saucepan, over low heat, melt chocolate chips with EAGLE BRAND®, remaining 1 1/2 teaspoons vanilla and salt. Remove from heat. Immediately spread over hot brownies. Cool. Chill. Cut into bars. Store covered at room temperature.

Makes 3 to 3 1/2 dozen brownies

Fudge Topped Brownies

Pink Peppermint Meringues

3 egg whites
$\frac{1}{8}$ teaspoon peppermint extract
5 drops red food coloring
$\frac{1}{2}$ cup superfine sugar*
6 peppermint candies, finely crushed

*Or, $\frac{1}{2}$ cup granulated sugar processed in food processor 1 minute until very fine.

1. Preheat oven to 200°F. Line 2 cookie sheets with parchment paper; set aside.

2. Beat egg whites in medium bowl with electric mixer at medium-high speed about 45 seconds or until frothy. Stir in peppermint extract and food coloring. Add sugar, 1 tablespoon at a time, while mixer is running. Continue beating until egg whites are stiff and glossy.

3. Drop meringue by teaspoonfuls into 1-inch mounds on prepared cookie sheets; sprinkle evenly with crushed peppermint candies.

4. Bake 2 hours or until meringues are dry when tapped. Transfer parchment paper with meringues to wire racks to cool completely. When cool, peel meringues off parchment; store in airtight container. *Makes about 74 meringues*

Pink Peppermint Meringues

203

Kookie Cookies

Basic Icebox Cookie Dough

- 1 cup butter or margarine, softened
- 1 cup sugar
- 1 egg
- 1 teaspoon vanilla
- 2 $^1/_2$ cups all-purpose flour
- 1 teaspoon baking powder
- $^1/_2$ teaspoon salt

Beat butter and sugar with an electric mixer. Add egg and vanilla; mix well. Combine flour, baking powder and salt. Gradually add to butter mixture; mix well.

Makes 4$^1/_2$ cups dough

Maraschino Cherry Cookies: Add $^1/_2$ cup chopped well-drained maraschino cherries to basic dough; divide dough in half. Form dough into 2 logs, 1$^1/_2$ inches in diameter. Wrap in waxed paper and refrigerate at least 6 hours. Cut into $^1/_4$-inch slices. Place 1 to 1$^1/_2$ inches apart on *ungreased* baking sheet. Bake in preheated 375°F oven 8 to 10 minutes. Remove to cooling rack. Repeat with remaining dough. Makes 6 to 7 dozen cookies.

Maraschino Thumbprint Cookies: Shape dough into balls, using 2 teaspoons dough for each cookie. Press thumb in center of each ball. Place whole well-drained maraschino cherry in center of each depression. Brush with beaten egg white. For a nutty variation, roll each dough ball in beaten egg white, then in finely chopped pecans before pressing with thumb and filling with cherry. Place 1 to 1$^1/_2$ inches apart on *ungreased* baking sheet. Bake in preheated 375°F 12 to 15 minutes. Remove to cooling rack. Makes 5 dozen cookies.

Maraschino Date Pinwheels: Combine 8 ounces chopped pitted dates and $^1/_4$ cup water in small saucepan; bring to a boil. Reduce heat;simmer until thickened. Add $^3/_4$ cup chopped drained maraschino cherries; mix well and cool. Divide dough in half. Roll out each half to 12×10-inch rectangle on lightly floured surface. Spread half of cooled filling on each rectangle. Roll up beginning at long ends. Pinch ends of rolls to seal.

Wrap in waxed paper and refrigerate at least 6 hours. Cut rolls into ¼-inch slices. Place 1 to 1½ inches apart on *ungreased* baking sheet. Bake in preheated 375°F oven about 10 to 14 minutes or until lightly browned. Remove to cooling rack. Makes 6 to 7 dozen cookies.

Favorite recipe from **Cherry Marketing Institute**

Original Nestlé® Toll House® Chocolate Chip Cookies

2 ¼ cups all-purpose flour
1 teaspoon baking soda
1 teaspoon salt
1 cup (2 sticks) butter, softened
¾ cup granulated sugar
¾ cup packed brown sugar
1 teaspoon vanilla extract
2 large eggs
2 cups (12-ounce package) NESTLÉ® TOLL HOUSE® Semi-Sweet Chocolate Morsels
1 cup chopped nuts

PREHEAT oven to 375°F.

COMBINE flour, baking soda and salt in small bowl. Beat butter, granulated sugar, brown sugar and vanilla extract in large mixer bowl until creamy. Add eggs, one at a time, beating well after each addition. Gradually beat in flour mixture. Stir in morsels and nuts. Drop by rounded tablespoonfuls onto ungreased baking sheets.

BAKE for 9 to 11 minutes or until golden brown. Cool on baking sheets for 2 minutes; remove to wire racks to cool completely.   *Makes about 5 dozen cookies*

Pan Cookie Variation: **GREASE** 15×10-inch jelly-roll pan. Prepare dough as above. Spread in prepared pan. Bake for 20 to 25 minutes or until golden brown. Cool in pan on wire rack. Makes 4 dozen bars.

Fruit and Nut Bars

- 1 cup unsifted all-purpose flour
- 1 cup uncooked quick oats
- 2/3 cup brown sugar
- 2 teaspoons baking soda
- 1/2 teaspoon salt
- 1/2 teaspoon ground cinnamon
- 2/3 cup buttermilk
- 3 tablespoons vegetable oil
- 2 egg whites, lightly beaten
- 1 Washington Golden Delicious apple, cored and chopped
- 1/2 cup dried cranberries or raisins, chopped
- 1/4 cup chopped nuts
- 2 tablespoons flaked coconut (optional)

1. Heat oven to 375°F. Lightly grease 9-inch square baking pan. In large mixing bowl, combine flour, oats, brown sugar, baking soda, salt and cinnamon; stir to blend.

2. Add buttermilk, oil and egg whites; beat with electric mixer just until mixed. Stir in apple, dried fruit and nuts; spread evenly in pan and top with coconut, if desired. Bake 20 to 25 minutes or until cake tester inserted in center comes out clean. Cool and cut into 16 bars.

Makes 16 bars

Favorite recipe from **Washington Apple Commission**

Chocolate Crackletops

2 cups all-purpose flour
2 teaspoons baking powder
2 cups granulated sugar
½ cup (**1** stick) butter or margarine
4 squares (**1** ounce each) unsweetened baking chocolate, chopped
4 large eggs, lightly beaten
2 teaspoons vanilla extract
1 ¾ cups "M&M's"® Chocolate Mini Baking Bits
Additional granulated sugar

Combine flour and baking powder; set aside. In 2-quart saucepan over medium heat combine 2 cups sugar, butter and chocolate, stirring until butter and chocolate are melted; remove from heat. Gradually stir in eggs and vanilla. Stir in flour mixture until well blended. Chill mixture 1 hour. Stir in "M&M's"® Chocolate Mini Baking Bits; chill mixture an additional 1 hour.

Preheat oven to 350°F. Line cookie sheets with foil. With sugar-dusted hands, roll dough into 1-inch balls; roll balls in additional granulated sugar. Place about 2 inches apart onto prepared cookie sheets. Bake 10 to 12 minutes. Do not overbake. Cool completely on wire racks. Store in tightly covered container.

Makes about 5 dozen cookies

Chocolate Crackletops

Kookie Cookies

Almond Chinese Chews

  1 cup granulated sugar
  3 eggs, lightly beaten
  1 can **SOLO**® or 1 jar **BAKER**® Almond Filling
  ³/₄ cup all-purpose flour
  1 teaspoon baking powder
  ¹/₄ teaspoon salt
    Powdered sugar

1. Preheat oven to 300°F. Grease 13×9-inch baking pan; set aside.

2. Beat granulated sugar and eggs in medium-size bowl with electric mixer until thoroughly blended. Add almond filling; beat until blended. Sift together flour, baking powder and salt; fold into almond mixture. Spread batter evenly in prepared pan.

3. Bake 40 to 45 minutes or until wooden toothpick inserted into center comes out clean. Cool completely in pan on wire rack. Cut into 2×1¹/₂-inch bars; dust with powdered sugar. *Makes about 3 dozen bars*

helpful hint:

Bar cookies can be cut into many attractive shapes. Cut the cookies into wide strips then slice on an angle to make diamonds or in a zigzag pattern for triangles.

Almond Chinese Chews

211

Christmas Spritz Cookies

2 ¼ cups all-purpose flour
¼ teaspoon salt
1 ¼ cups powdered sugar
1 cup (2 sticks) butter, softened
1 egg
1 teaspoon almond extract
1 teaspoon vanilla
Green food coloring (optional)
Icing (recipe follows, optional)
Candied red and green cherries and assorted decorative candies (optional)

1. Preheat oven to 375°F. Combine flour and salt in medium bowl. Combine powdered sugar and butter in large bowl; beat with electric mixer at medium speed until light and fluffy. Beat in egg, almond extract and vanilla. Gradually add flour mixture. Beat until well blended.

2. Divide dough in half. Tint half of dough with green food coloring, if desired. Fit cookie press with desired plate. Fill press with dough; press dough 1 inch apart onto ungreased cookie sheets.

3. Bake 10 to 12 minutes or until just set. Remove cookies to wire racks; cool completely.

4. Prepare Icing, if desired; pipe or drizzle onto cooled cookies. Decorate with cherries and assorted candies. Store tightly covered at room temperature or freeze up to 3 months. *Makes about 5 dozen cookies*

Icing

1 ½ **cups powdered sugar**
  2 **tablespoons milk plus additional, if needed**
 ⅛ **teaspoon almond extract**

Place all ingredients in medium bowl; stir until thick but spreadable. (If icing is too thick, stir in 1 teaspoon additional milk.)

Quick and Easy Jumbles

  1 **package (about 17 ounces) sugar cookie mix**
½ **cup (1 stick) butter, melted**
  1 **egg, lightly beaten**
½ **cup mini candy-coated chocolate pieces or semisweet chocolate chips**
½ **cup raisins**
½ **cup coarsely chopped walnuts**

1. Preheat oven to 350°F.

2. Combine cookie mix, butter and egg in large bowl. Stir with spoon until well blended. Stir in chocolate pieces, raisins and walnuts.

3. Drop dough by rounded teaspoonfuls onto *ungreased* cookie sheets about 2 inches apart. Bake for 7 to 8 minutes or until set. Cool 1 minute on cookie sheets. Remove cookies to wire racks; cool completely.   *Makes about 2 dozen cookies*

Hershey's "Perfectly Chocolate" Chocolate Chip Cookies

- 1 cup (2 sticks) butter or margarine, softened
- ³/₄ cup granulated sugar
- ³/₄ cup packed light brown sugar
- 1 teaspoon vanilla extract
- 2 eggs
- 2¹/₄ cups all-purpose flour
- ¹/₃ cup HERSHEY'S Cocoa
- 1 teaspoon baking soda
- ¹/₂ teaspoon salt
- 2 cups (12-ounce package) HERSHEY'S Semi-Sweet Chocolate Chips
- 1 cup chopped nuts (optional)

1. Heat oven to 375°F.

2. Beat butter, granulated sugar, brown sugar and vanilla in large bowl until creamy. Add eggs; beat well. Stir together flour, cocoa, baking soda and salt; gradually add to butter mixture, beating until well blended. Stir in chocolate chips and nuts, if desired. Drop by rounded teaspoons onto ungreased cookie sheet.

3. Bake 8 to 10 minutes or until set. Cool slightly; remove from cookie sheet to wire rack. Cool completely. *Makes about 5 dozen cookies*

Hershey®'s "Perfectly Chocolate" Chocolate Chip Cookies

Oatmeal Cookies

 1 cup all-purpose flour
 1 teaspoon baking powder
 $1/2$ teaspoon baking soda
 $1/2$ teaspoon salt
 $1/4$ cup MOTT'S® Cinnamon Apple Sauce
 2 tablespoons margarine
 $1/2$ cup granulated sugar
 $1/2$ cup firmly packed light brown sugar
 1 egg *or* $1/4$ cup egg substitute
 1 teaspoon vanilla extract
 1 $1/3$ cups uncooked rolled oats
 $1/2$ cup raisins (optional)

Heat oven to 375°F. Lightly spray cookie sheet with cooking spray. In large bowl, mix flour, baking powder, baking soda and salt. In separate bowl, beat together apple sauce, margarine, granulated and brown sugars, egg and vanilla until margarine forms pea-sized pieces. Add flour mixture to apple sauce mixture. Mix well. Fold in oats and raisins. Drop rounded teaspoonfuls of dough onto cookie sheet; bake 5 minutes. Remove cookies from cookie sheet and cool completely on wire rack.

Makes 36 cookies

Top to bottom: Oatmeal Cookies and Gingersnaps (page 198)

217

Coconut Macaroons

- 1 (14-ounce) can **EAGLE BRAND**® Sweetened Condensed Milk (**NOT** evaporated milk)
- 1 egg white, whipped
- 2 teaspoons vanilla extract
- 1 1/2 teaspoons almond extract
- 1 (14-ounce) package flaked coconut

1. Preheat oven to 325°F. Line baking sheets with foil; grease and flour foil. Set aside.

2. In large bowl, combine EAGLE BRAND®, egg white, extracts and coconut; mix well. Drop by rounded teaspoonfuls onto prepared baking sheets; slightly flatten each mound with a spoon.

3. Bake 15 to 17 minutes or until lightly browned around edges. Immediately remove from baking sheets (macaroons will stick if allowed to cool); cool on wire racks. Store loosely covered at room temperature.   *Makes about 4 dozen cookies*

Prep Time: 10 minutes
Bake Time: 15 to 17 minutes

helpful hint:

Crunchy on the outside and moist and chewy on the inside, these sweets are perfect for an afternoon sugar fix. They are quick and easy to make and look especially attractive on a cookie tray.

Coconut Macaroons

Rocky Road Brownies

1 ¼ cups miniature marshmallows
1 cup **HERSHEY'S** Semi-Sweet Chocolate Chips
½ cup chopped nuts
½ cup (1 stick) butter or margarine
1 cup sugar
2 eggs
1 teaspoon vanilla extract
½ cup all-purpose flour
1/3 cup **HERSHEY'S** Cocoa
½ teaspoon baking powder
½ teaspoon salt

1. Heat oven to 350°F. Grease 9-inch square baking pan.

2. Stir together marshmallows, chocolate chips and nuts; set aside. Place butter in large microwave-safe bowl. Microwave at HIGH (100%) 1 to 1 ½ minutes or until melted. Add sugar, eggs and vanilla, beating with spoon until well blended. Add flour, cocoa, baking powder and salt; blend well. Spread batter in prepared pan.

3. Bake 22 minutes. Sprinkle chocolate chip mixture over top. Continue baking 5 minutes or until marshmallows have softened and puffed slightly. Cool completely. With wet knife, cut into squares. *Makes about 20 brownies*

Rocky Road Brownies

Dainty Desserts

America has always had quite a sweet tooth, and in

the '50s with sugar rationing over, it was time to indulge.

Tastes had become more international and "gourmet"

since people were traveling abroad in record numbers.

Fancy desserts, preferably those that could

be set on fire, were very popular. Crêpes Suzettes

and Bananas Flambé are still delicious and impressive.

(Just keep the fire extinguisher handy.)

Sweetheart Chocolate Mousse (page 232)

Brandied Peaches & Cream

1 1/4 cups packed brown sugar
2/3 cup light corn syrup
1/4 cup (1/2 stick) butter
6 medium peaches, peeled, pitted and quartered*
1/2 cup heavy cream
1/2 cup brandy, divided
1/2 teaspoon vanilla
Vanilla ice cream

*If fresh peaches aren't available, replace with peeled, cored and quartered apples.

1. Combine brown sugar, corn syrup and butter in large skillet over medium-high heat, stirring to dissolve sugar. Cook 2 to 3 minutes. Add peaches, cream, 1/4 cup brandy and vanilla. Cook, stirring frequently, until peaches are very soft, about 15 minutes.

2. Add remaining 1/4 cup brandy to peach mixture and carefully light with a long match to flambé. Cook until flames go out; turn off heat. Serve sauce with peaches over vanilla ice cream. *Makes 8 servings*

Brandied Peaches & Cream

Chocolate Orange Meringues

   3 egg whites
   $1/2$ teaspoon vanilla extract
   $1/8$ teaspoon orange extract
   $3/4$ cup sugar
   $1/4$ cup HERSHEY'S Cocoa
   $1/2$ teaspoon freshly grated orange peel

1. Heat oven to 300°F. Cover cookie sheet with parchment paper or foil.

2. Beat egg whites, vanilla and orange extract in large bowl on high speed of mixer until soft peaks form. Gradually add sugar, beating well after each addition until stiff peaks hold their shape, sugar is dissolved and mixture is glossy. Sprinkle half of cocoa and all of orange peel over egg white mixture; gently fold in just until combined. Repeat with remaining cocoa.

3. Spoon mixture into pastry bag fitted with large star tip; pipe 1 $1/2$-inch-diameter stars onto prepared cookie sheet.

4. Bake 35 to 40 minutes or until dry. Cool slightly; peel paper from cookies. Cool completely on wire rack. Store, covered, at room temperature.

Makes 5 dozen cookies

Chocolate Orange Meringues

Creamy Banana Pudding

1 (14-ounce) can **EAGLE BRAND®** Sweetened Condensed Milk (**NOT** evaporated milk)
1 ½ cups cold water
1 (4-serving-size) package instant vanilla pudding and pie filling mix
2 cups (1 pint) whipping cream, whipped
36 vanilla wafers
3 medium bananas, sliced and dipped in lemon juice

1. In large bowl, combine EAGLE BRAND® and water. Add pudding mix; beat until well blended. Chill 5 minutes.

2. Fold in whipped cream. Spoon 1 cup pudding mixture into 2½-quart glass serving bowl or divide it among 8 to 10 individual serving dishes.

3. Top with one-third each of vanilla wafers, bananas and pudding mixture. Repeat layering twice, ending with pudding mixture. Chill. Garnish as desired. Store leftovers covered in refrigerator.   *Makes 8 to 10 servings*

Prep Time: 15 minutes

helpful hint:

Dipping banana slices in lemon juice helps to keep them from browning. Don't worry—the bananas won't have a lemon flavor.

Creamy Banana Pudding

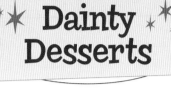

Dainty Desserts

Crêpes Suzette

>   **Crêpes (recipe follows)**
>   **Orange marmalade or pineapple fruit spread**
> **5 tablespoons butter, divided**
> **10 tablespoons orange-flavored liqueur**

1. Prepare Crêpes; cool to room temperature.

2. Spread each crêpe with marmalade; fold in half. Melt 1 tablespoon butter in medium skillet over medium heat. Add 2 filled crêpes; cook 2 minutes. Turn; cook 1 minute more.

3. Drizzle with 2 tablespoons liqueur; remove from heat. Carefully ignite with a long match; shake skillet until flames are extinguished. Transfer crêpes to warm serving plate; top with sauce. Repeat with remaining filled crêpes. Serve immediately.

Makes 5 servings

Crêpes

> **¾ cup all-purpose flour**
> **¾ cup milk**
> **2 eggs**
> **1 tablespoon butter, melted, divided**

1. Combine flour, milk, eggs and 1 tablespoon butter in food processor or blender; cover and process until smooth. Let stand at room temperature 1 hour or cover and refrigerate up to 8 hours.

2. Process batter to combine again just before cooking. Heat 5- or 6-inch crêpe pan over medium heat; lightly brush with remaining melted butter. Pour scant ¼ cup batter into hot pan; tilt and rotate pan to spread batter. Cook 1 or 2 minutes until crêpe is lightly browned around edges and top is dry. Turn and cook 30 seconds; slide onto sheet of waxed paper. Repeat with remaining batter. *Makes 10 crêpes*

Crêpes Suzette

231

Sweetheart Chocolate Mousse

    1 envelope unflavored gelatin
    2 tablespoons cold water
    ¼ cup boiling water
    1 cup sugar
    ½ cup HERSHEY'S Cocoa
    2 cups (1 pint) cold whipping cream
    2 teaspoons vanilla extract
      Fresh raspberries or sliced strawberries

1. Sprinkle gelatin over cold water in small bowl; let stand 2 minutes to soften. Add boiling water; stir until gelatin is completely dissolved and mixture is clear. Cool slightly.

2. Mix sugar and cocoa in large bowl; add whipping cream and vanilla. Beat on medium speed, scraping bottom of bowl occasionally, until mixture is stiff. Pour in gelatin mixture; beat until well blended.

3. Spoon into dessert dishes. Refrigerate at least 30 minutes before serving. Garnish with fruit.
Makes about 8 servings

Classic English Toffee

1 cup (2 sticks) unsalted butter
1 cup sugar
2 tablespoons water
$^1/_4$ teaspoon salt
1 teaspoon vanilla
3 squares (1 ounce each) semisweet chocolate
3 squares (1 ounce each) bittersweet chocolate
$^1/_2$ cup chopped toasted pecans

1. Line 9-inch square pan with heavy-duty foil, leaving 1-inch overhang on all sides.

2. Combine butter, sugar, water and salt in heavy 2- or 2$^1/_2$-quart saucepan. Bring to a boil over medium heat, stirring frequently. Attach candy thermometer to side of pan. Continue boiling about 20 minutes or until sugar mixture reaches hard-crack stage (305° to 310°F) on candy thermometer, stirring frequently. (Watch closely after temperature reaches 290°F. Temperature will rise quickly and mixture will burn above 310°F.) Remove from heat; stir in vanilla. Immediately pour into prepared pan, spreading to edges. Cool completely.

3. Microwave chocolates in small microwavable bowl on MEDIUM (50%) 5 to 6 minutes or until melted, stirring every 2 minutes.

4. Spread chocolate evenly over toffee. Sprinkle chocolate with pecans. Refrigerate about 35 minutes or until chocolate is set. Bring to room temperature before breaking toffee.

5. Carefully break toffee into pieces without dislodging pecans. Store in airtight container at room temperature between sheets of waxed paper.

Makes about 1$^1/_4$ pounds toffee

Tip: Toffee makes an excellent homemade gift. It's simple to make it even more special by creating a unique gift box. Decorate an unfinished papier mâché or wood box with acrylic paints, markers, stamps or fabric. Line the box with coordinating tissue paper and wrap it with matching ribbon.

Dainty Desserts

Chocolate Petits Fours

- 1 package **DUNCAN HINES**® Moist Deluxe® Dark Chocolate Fudge Cake Mix
- 1 package (7 ounces) pure almond paste
- 1/2 cup seedless red raspberry jam
- 3 cups semisweet chocolate chips
- 1/2 cup vegetable shortening plus additional for greasing

1. Preheat oven to 350°F. Grease and flour 13×9-inch pan. Prepare, bake and cool cake following package directions for basic recipe. Remove from pan. Level top of cake. Trim 1/4-inch strip of cake from all sides. (Be careful to make straight cuts.) Cut cake into small squares, rectangles or triangles with serrated knife. Cut round and heart shapes with 1 1/2- to 2-inch cookie cutters. Split each individual cake horizontally into two layers.

2. For filling, cut almond paste in half. Roll half the paste between two sheets of waxed paper to 1/8-inch thickness. Cut into same shapes as individual cakes. Repeat with second half of paste. Warm jam in small saucepan over low heat until thin. Remove top of one cake. Spread 1/4 to 1/2 teaspoon jam on inside of each cut surface. Place one almond paste cutout on bottom layer. Top with second half of cake, jam side down. Repeat with remaining cakes.

3. For glaze, place chocolate chips and 1/2 cup shortening in 4-cup glass measuring cup. Microwave at MEDIUM (50% power) for 2 minutes; stir. Microwave for 2 minutes longer at MEDIUM; stir until smooth. Place 3 assembled cakes on cooling rack over bowl. Spoon chocolate glaze over each cake until top and sides are completely covered. Remove to waxed paper when glaze has stopped dripping. Repeat process until all cakes are covered. (Return chocolate glaze in bowl to glass measuring cup as needed; microwave at MEDIUM for 30 to 60 seconds to thin.)

4. Place remaining chocolate glaze in resealable plastic bag; seal. Place bag in bowl of hot water for several minutes. Dry with paper towel. Knead until chocolate is smooth. Snip pinpoint hole in bottom corner of bag. Drizzle or decorate top of each petit four. Let stand until chocolate is set. Store in single layer in airtight containers.

Makes 24 to 32 servings

Chocolate Petits Fours

Rice Pudding

1 1/4 cups water, divided
1/2 cup uncooked long-grain rice
2 cups evaporated skim milk
1/2 cup granulated sugar
1/2 cup raisins
1/2 cup MOTT'S® Natural Apple Sauce
3 tablespoons cornstarch
1 teaspoon vanilla extract
Brown sugar or nutmeg (optional)
Fresh raspberries (optional)
Orange peel strips (optional)

1. In medium saucepan, bring 1 cup water to a boil. Add rice. Reduce heat to low and simmer, covered, 20 minutes or until rice is tender and water is absorbed.

2. Add milk, granulated sugar, raisins and apple sauce. Bring to a boil. Reduce heat to low and simmer for 3 minutes, stirring occasionally.

3. Combine cornstarch and remaining 1/4 cup water in small bowl. Stir into rice mixture. Simmer about 20 minutes or until mixture thickens, stirring occasionally. Remove from heat; stir in vanilla. Cool 15 to 20 minutes before serving. Sprinkle each serving with brown sugar or nutmeg and garnish with raspberries and orange peel, if desired. Refrigerate leftovers. *Makes 8 servings*

Rice Pudding

Toll House® Famous Fudge

1 ½ cups granulated sugar
²/₃ cup (5 fluid-ounce can) **NESTLÉ® CARNATION®** Evaporated Milk
2 tablespoons butter or margarine
¼ teaspoon salt
2 cups miniature marshmallows
1 ½ cups (9 ounces) **NESTLÉ® TOLL HOUSE®** Semi-Sweet Chocolate Morsels
½ cup chopped pecans or walnuts (optional)
1 teaspoon vanilla extract

LINE 8-inch-square baking pan with foil.

COMBINE sugar, evaporated milk, butter and salt in medium, *heavy-duty* saucepan. Bring to a *full rolling boil* over medium heat, stirring constantly. Boil, stirring constantly, for 4 to 5 minutes. Remove from heat.

STIR in marshmallows, morsels, nuts and vanilla extract. Stir vigorously for 1 minute or until marshmallows are melted. Pour into prepared baking pan; refrigerate for 2 hours or until firm. Lift from pan; remove foil. Cut into pieces.

Makes 49 pieces

For Milk Chocolate Fudge: **SUBSTITUTE** 1 ¾ cups (11.5-ounce package) NESTLÉ® TOLL HOUSE® Milk Chocolate Morsels for Semi-Sweet Morsels.

For Butterscotch Fudge: **SUBSTITUTE** 1 ²/₃ cups (11-ounce package) NESTLÉ® TOLL HOUSE® Butterscotch Flavored Morsels for Semi-Sweet Morsels.

For Peanutty Chocolate Fudge: **SUBSTITUTE** 1 ²/₃ cups (11-ounce package) NESTLÉ® TOLL HOUSE® Peanut Butter & Milk Chocolate Morsels for Semi-Sweet Morsels and ½ cup chopped peanuts for pecans or walnuts.

Toll House® Famous Fudge

Creamy Baked Cheesecake

1 1/4 cups graham cracker crumbs

1/4 cup sugar

1/3 cup (2/3 stick) butter, melted

2 (8-ounce) packages cream cheese, softened

1 (14-ounce) can EAGLE BRAND® Sweetened Condensed Milk (NOT evaporated milk)

3 eggs

1/4 cup lemon juice

1 (8-ounce) container sour cream, at room temperature

Raspberry Topping (optional recipe follows)

1. Preheat oven to 300°F. In small bowl, combine graham cracker crumbs, sugar and butter; press firmly on bottom of ungreased 9-inch springform pan.

2. In large bowl, beat cream cheese until fluffy. Gradually beat in EAGLE BRAND® until smooth. Add eggs and lemon juice; mix well. Pour into prepared crust.

3. Bake 50 to 55 minutes or until set. Remove from oven; top with sour cream. Bake 5 minutes longer. Cool. Chill. Prepare Raspberry Topping (optional) and serve with cheesecake. Store leftovers covered in refrigerator.

Makes one (9-inch) cheesecake

Prep Time: 25 minutes
Bake Time: 55 to 60 minutes
Chill Time: 4 hours

Raspberry Topping

2 cups water
¼ cup red raspberry jam
8 tablespoons confectioners' sugar
1 tablespoon cornstarch
1 cup frozen red raspberries

In small saucepan combine water, red raspberry jam, confectioners' sugar and cornstarch. Cook and stir until thickened and clear. Cool. Stir in raspberries.

New York Style Cheesecake: Increase cream cheese to 4 (8-ounce) packages and eggs to 4. Proceed as directed, adding 2 tablespoons flour after eggs. Bake 1 hour 10 minutes or until center is set. Omit sour cream. Cool. Chill. Serve and store as directed.

Bananas Flambé

2 tablespoons butter
½ teaspoon ground cinnamon
2 small firm ripe bananas, peeled and cut in half lengthwise
2 tablespoons frozen unsweetened apple juice concentrate
2 tablespoons brandy or cognac

Melt butter in 10-inch skillet over medium heat. Stir in cinnamon. Add bananas; cook until thoroughly heated, about 1 minute per side. Add apple juice concentrate; cook 1 minute, stirring occasionally. Drizzle with brandy; remove from heat. Carefully ignite with lighted match. Carefully shake skillet until flames are extinguished. Transfer bananas to individual dessert dishes, reserving liquid in skillet. Cook liquid over medium-high heat until thickened and bubbly, about 1 minute. Pour over bananas; serve immediately.

Makes 2 servings

Peach Tapioca

2 cups milk
3 tablespoons quick-cooking tapioca
1 egg, lightly beaten
1 ½ cups peeled, coarsely chopped peaches*
3 tablespoons apricot fruit spread
1 teaspoon vanilla

*If fresh peaches are not in season, use frozen peaches and add 4 teaspoons sugar to milk mixture.

1. Combine milk, tapioca and egg in 1 ½-quart saucepan; let stand 5 minutes. Stir in peaches and apricot spread.

2. Cook and stir over medium heat until mixture comes to a rolling boil; cook 1 minute more. Remove from heat and stir in vanilla.

3. Cool slightly; stir. Place plastic wrap directly on surface of pudding; chill.

Makes 4 servings

helpful hint:

Peeling peaches is easier if you first plunge them into boiling water for about 1 minute. You can then rub the skin off with your fingers or a paper towel.

Peach Tapioca

Dainty Desserts

Fruit-Filled Chocolate Chip Meringue Nests

MERINGUES

- 4 large egg whites
- 1/2 teaspoon salt
- 1/2 teaspoon cream of tartar
- 1 cup granulated sugar
- 2 cups (12-ounce package) NESTLÉ® TOLL HOUSE® Semi-Sweet Chocolate Morsels

CHOCOLATE SAUCE

- 2/3 cup (5 fluid-ounce can) NESTLÉ® CARNATION® Evaporated Milk
- 1 cup (6 ounces) NESTLÉ® TOLL HOUSE® Semi-Sweet Chocolate Morsels
- 1 tablespoon granulated sugar
- 1 teaspoon vanilla extract
  Pinch salt
- 3 cups fresh fruit or berries (whole blackberries, blueberries or raspberries, sliced kiwi, peaches or strawberries)

FOR MERINGUES

PREHEAT oven to 300°F. Lightly grease baking sheets.

BEAT egg whites, salt and cream of tartar in large mixer bowl until soft peaks form. Gradually add sugar; beat until sugar is dissolved. Gently fold in morsels. Spread meringue into ten 3-inch nests with deep wells about 2 inches apart on prepared baking sheets.

BAKE for 35 to 45 minutes or until meringues are dry and crisp. Cool on baking sheets for 5 minutes; remove to wire racks to cool completely.

FOR CHOCOLATE SAUCE

HEAT evaporated milk to a boil in small, *heavy-duty* saucepan. Stir in morsels. Cook, stirring constantly, until mixture is slightly thickened and smooth. Remove from heat; stir in sugar, vanilla extract and salt.

FILL meringues with fruit and drizzle with Chocolate Sauce; serve immediately.

Makes 10 servings

Fruit-Filled Chocolate Chip Meringue Nests

245

Hot Fudge Pudding Cake

1 1/4 cups granulated sugar, divided
1 cup all-purpose flour
1/2 cup **HERSHEY'S** Cocoa, divided
2 teaspoons baking powder
1/4 teaspoon salt
1/2 cup milk
1/3 cup butter or margarine, melted
1 1/2 teaspoons vanilla extract
1/2 cup packed light brown sugar
1 1/4 cups hot water
Whipped topping

1. Heat oven to 350°F.

2. Stir together 3/4 cup granulated sugar, flour, 1/4 cup cocoa, baking powder and salt. Stir in milk, butter and vanilla; beat until smooth. Pour batter into ungreased 9-inch square baking pan. Stir together remaining 1/2 cup granulated sugar, brown sugar and remaining 1/4 cup cocoa; sprinkle mixture evenly over batter. Pour hot water over top. Do not stir.

3. Bake 35 to 40 minutes or until center is almost set. Let stand 15 minutes; spoon into dessert dishes, spooning sauce from bottom of pan over top. Garnish with whipped topping. *Makes about 8 servings*

Prep Time: 10 minutes
Bake Time: 35 minutes
Cool Time: 15 minutes

Hot Fudge Pudding Cake

Candied Orange Peel

8 to 10 medium thick-skinned oranges, washed
Water
1 teaspoon salt
2 cups sugar
1 cup water
1/2 cup **KARO**® Light Corn Syrup
Sugar
Melted semisweet chocolate (optional)

1. Cut oranges just through peel into quarters; remove peel and place in large saucepan. (Reserve oranges for eating or for use in salads and fruit cups.)

2. Cover orange peel with cold water; add salt. Bring to boil; boil 10 minutes. Drain. Boil and drain 2 more times, omitting salt.

3. Gently scrape off moist white membrane with spoon. (Peel should be about 1/4 inch thick.) Cut peel into 1/4-inch-wide strips.

4. In 3-quart saucepan combine 2 cups sugar, 1 cup water and corn syrup. Stirring constantly, cook over medium heat until sugar is dissolved. Add orange peel. Bring to boil; reduce heat and boil gently 45 minutes. Drain well.

5. A few pieces at a time, roll orange peel in sugar. Arrange in single layer on wire racks. Let dry, lightly covered, in warm place 10 to 12 hours. Store in covered container.

6. If desired, dip 1 end in melted chocolate. Place on waxed paper-lined cookie sheet. Chill 15 minutes or until set.

Makes about 8 cups

Prep Time: 2 hours, plus drying

Acknowledgments

The publisher would like to thank the companies and organizations listed below for the use of their recipes and photographs in this publication.

ACH Food Companies, Inc.
Bob Evans®
California Tree Fruit Agreement
Cherry Marketing Institute
Clamato® is a registered trademark of Mott's, LLP
Delmarva Poultry Industry, Inc.
Del Monte Corporation
Dole Food Company, Inc.
Duncan Hines® and Moist Deluxe® are registered trademarks of Pinnacle Foods Corp.
EAGLE BRAND®
Florida Department of Agriculture and Consumer Services, Bureau of Seafood and Aquaculture
Grandma's® is a registered trademark of Mott's, LLP
The Hershey Company
Hillshire Farm®
Holland House® is a registered trademark of Mott's, LLP
Hormel Foods, LLC
The Kingsford® Products Co.
© Mars, Incorporated 2007
McIlhenny Company (TABASCO® brand Pepper Sauce)
Minnesota Cultivated Wild Rice Council
Mott's® is a registered trademark of Mott's, LLP
National Cattlemen's Beef Association on Behalf of The Beef Checkoff
National Pork Board
Nestlé USA
Reckitt Benckiser Inc.
Sokol and Company
StarKist Seafood Company
Unilever
Veg•All®
Washington Apple Commission
Wisconsin Milk Marketing Board

Index

A

All-American Burger, The, 156
Almond Chinese Chews, 210
Ambrosia, 122

B

Banana
    Ambrosia, 122
    Bananas Flambé, 241
    Creamy Banana Pudding, 228
    Spiced Grilled Bananas, 124
Basic Crêpes, 81
Basic Icebox Cookie Dough, 204
Beef (*see also* **Beef, Ground; Veal**),
    32–59
    Cavemen Beef Back Ribs, 154
    Drunken T-Bone Steak, 158
    Espresso-Bourbon Steaks with Mashed
      Sweet Potatoes, 150
    Grilled T-Bone Steaks With BBQ Rub,
      142
    Marinated Flank Steak with Pineapple,
      146
    Mixed Grill Kabobs, 148
    Surf & Turf Kabobs, 162
Beef, Ground
    All-American Burger, The 156
    Beef Stroganoff Casserole, 102
    Blue Cheese Burgers with Red Onion,
      144
    Cheeseburger Macaroni, 94
    Hawaiian-Style Burgers, 136
    Hearty Shepherd's Pie, 97
    Souperior Meat Loaf, 54
    Swedish Meatballs, 48
    Tamale Pie, 105
    Veg•All® Beef & Cheddar Bake, 96
Beef Stroganoff, 58
Beef Stroganoff Casserole, 102
Beef Wellington, 50

Blueberry Angel Food Cake Rolls, 188
Blue Cheese Burgers with Red Onion, 144
Blue Crab Stuffed Tomatoes, 18
Brandied Peaches & Cream, 224
Brandy-Soaked Scallops, 14
Brownies
    Fudge Topped Brownies, 200
    Rocky Road Brownies, 220
Bundt Cakes
    Fudge Ribbon Bundt Cake, 170
    Pumpkin Pecan Rum Cake, 174
Burger Spread, 157
Butterscotch Fudge, 238

C

Cake Mix
    Blueberry Angel Food Cake Rolls, 188
    Chocolate Petit Fours, 234
    Fudge Ribbon Bundt Cake, 170
    Fudge Ribbon Cake, 170
    Mini Neopolitan Ice Cream Cakes, 182
    Pineapple Upside-Down Cake, 180
    Pretty-in-Pink Peppermint Cupcakes,
      172
    Strawberry Stripe Refrigerator Cake,
      192
    Tropical Luau Cupcakes, 134
California Bacon Dip, 22
California Blue Cheese Dip, 22
California Seafood Dip, 22
Candied Orange Peel, 248
Candy
    Butterscotch Fudge, 238
    Candied Orange Peel, 248
    Classic English Toffee, 233
    Milk Chocolate Fudge, 238
    Peanutty Chocolate Fudge, 238
    Toll House® Famous Fudge, 238
Caribbean Fruited Pork Roast, 120
Carmen Miranda Cake, 168

Index

Carolina-Style Barbecue Chicken, 152
Cavemen Beef Back Ribs, 154
Cheddar Cheese Spread, 27
Cheeseburger Macaroni, 94
Chicken, 60–87
    Carolina-Style Barbecue Chicken, 152
    Chicken, Asparagus & Mushroom Bake, 112
    Chicken Divan Casserole, 100
    Chicken Tetrazzini, 106
    Garlic & Lemon Herb Marinated Chicken, 164
    Hula Chicken Salad with Orange Poppy Seed Dressing, 132
    Wild Hawaiian Cocktail Meatballs, 17
    Zesty Liver Pâté, 26
Chicken and Broccoli Crêpes, 80
Chicken Bourguignonne, 71
Chicken Breasts Smothered in Tomatoes and Mozzarella, 82
Chicken Cordon Bleu, 78
Chicken Fricasee, 74
Chicken Wellington, 86
Chicken with Brandied Fruit Sauce, 72
Chicken with Peach-Champagne Sauce, 84
Chiffon Cakes
    Chocolate Chiffon Cake, 178
    Chocolate Orange Marble Chiffon Cake, 186
Chocolate Chiffon Cake, 178
Chocolate Crackletops, 208
Chocolate Glaze, 170
Chocolate Orange Marble Chiffon Cake, 186
Chocolate Orange Meringues, 226
Chocolate Petit Fours, 234
Christmas Spritz Cookies, 212
Chunky Hawaiian Spread, 118
Classic Chicken Marsala, 68
Classic English Toffee, 233

Classic Turkey Pot Pie, 92
Coconut
    Ambrosia, 122
    Coconut Macaroons, 218
    Coconut Pecan Frosting, 177
    Creamy Coconut-Lime Fruit Salad, 118
Coconut Macaroons, 218
Coconut Pecan Frosting, 177
Coq au Vin, 66
Country Sausage Macaroni and Cheese, 104
Crab and Artichoke Stuffed Mushrooms, 12
Crabmeat
    Blue Crab Stuffed Tomatoes, 18
    Crab and Artichoke Stuffed Mushrooms, 12
    Molded Crab Mousse, 10
    Seafood Newburg Casserole, 108
Creamy Baked Cheesecake, 240
Creamy Banana Pudding, 228
Creamy Coconut-Lime Fruit Salad, 118
Crêpes
    Basic Crêpes, 81
    Chicken and Broccoli Crêpes, 80
    Crêpes, 230
    Crêpes Suzette, 230
Crunchy Veg•All® Tuna Casserole, 92

D

Dips & Spreads
    Burger Spread, 157
    California Bacon Dip, 22
    California Blue Cheese Dip, 22
    California Seafood Dip, 22
    Cheddar Cheese Spread, 27
    Chunky Hawaiian Spread, 118
    Famous Lipton® California Dip, The, 22
    Molded Crab Mousse, 10
    Pecan Cheese Ball, 20

Index

Dips & Spreads (*continued*)
Sensational Spinach Dip, 22
Spicy Spam™ Party Dip, 16
Tuna Mushroom Pâté with Orange
   Liqueur, 28
Zesty Liver Pâté, 26
Double Cheese Veal Cutlets, 34
Down-Home Pork and Beans, 38
Drunken T-Bone Steak, 158

E
Espresso-Bourbon Steaks with Mashed
   Sweet Potatoes, 150

F
Famous Lipton® California Dip, The, 22
Filet Mignon with Tarragon Butter, 46
Filling (Lady Baltimore Cake), 185
French Bistro Ham, 42
Frosting (Lady Baltimore Cake), 185
Fruit and Nut Bars, 206
Fruit-Filled Chocolate Chip Meringue
   Nests, 244
Fudge Ribbon Bundt Cake, 170
Fudge Ribbon Cake, 170
Fudge Topped Brownies, 200

G
Garlic & Lemon Herb Marinated Chicken,
   164
German Chocolate Cake, 176
Gingersnaps, 198
Golden Glazed Flank Steak, 51
Grandma's Gingerbread, 177
Grilled Sherry Pork Chops, 157
Grilled T-Bone Steaks With BBQ Rub,
   142
Grill Recipes, 138–165
Hawaiian Ribs, 130
Hawaiian-Style Burgers, 136

Grill Recipes (*continued*)
South Seas Shrimp & Mango, 126
Spiced Grilled Bananas, 124

H
Ham & Canned Meat
French Bistro Ham, 42
Spam® à la King, 52
Spam™ Cornbread Pie, 94
Spam™ Hawaiian Pizza, 116
Spicy Spam™ Party Dip, 16
Hawaiian Ribs, 130
Hawaiian-Style Burgers, 136
Hearty Shepherd's Pie, 97
Herb Orange Pork Chops, 160
Hershey®'s "Perfectly Chocolate "
   Chocolate Chip Cookies, 214
Hershey®'s Red Velvet Cake, 190
Homestyle Chicken Pot Pie, 70
Hot Fudge Pudding Cake, 246
Hula Chicken Salad with Orange Poppy
   Seed Dressing, 132
Hungarian Beef Goulash, 44
Hungarian Goulash Casserole, 110

I
Icing (Christmas Spritz Cookies), 213

J
Javanese Pork Saté, 149

K
Kabobs
Javanese Pork Saté, 149
Mixed Grill Kabobs, 148
Surf & Turf Kabobs, 162

L
Lady Baltimore Cake, 184
Luscious Lemon Bars, 106

Index

M

Manhattan Turkey à la King, 62
Maraschino Cherry Cookies, 204
Maraschino Date Pinwheels, 204
Maraschino Thumbprint Cookies, 204
Marinated Flank Steak with Pineapple, 146

Marshmallows
Ambrosia, 122
Butterscotch Fudge, 238
Milk Chocolate Fudge, 238
Rocky Road Brownies, 220
Toll House® Famous Fudge, 238
Mashed Sweet Potatoes, 150

Meatballs
Swedish Meatballs, 48
Wild Hawaiian Cocktail Meatballs, 17

Meat Loaf: Souperior Meat Loaf, 54

Meringues
Chocolate Orange Meringues, 226
Fruit-Filled Chocolate Chip Meringue Nests, 244
Pink Peppermint Meringues, 202
Milk Chocolate Fudge, 238
Mini Neopolitan Ice Cream Cakes, 182
Mixed Grill Kabobs, 148
Molded Crab Mousse, 10

Mousse & Pudding
Creamy Banana Pudding, 228
Hot Fudge Pudding Cake, 246
Peach Tapioca, 242
Rice Pudding, 236
Sweetheart Chocolate Mousse, 232
Tidal Wave Cocoa Almond Mousse, 128

Mushrooms
Beef Stroganoff, 58
Beef Stroganoff Casserole, 102

Mushrooms *(continued)*
Beef Wellington, 50
Chicken, Asparagus & Mushroom Bake, 112
Chicken Bourguignonne, 71
Chicken Wellington, 86
Coq au Vin, 66
Country Sausage Macaroni and Cheese, 104
Crab and Artichoke Stuffed Mushrooms, 12
Manhattan Turkey à la King, 62
Salmon Casserole, 90
Tuna Mushroom Pâté with Orange Liqueur, 28
Veal Scallopini, 56
Venetian Canapés, 30

N

New York Style Cheesecake, 241

O

Oatmeal Cookies, 216
Orange Glaze, 188
Original Nestlé® Toll House® Chocolate Chip Cookies, 205
Oysters: Oysters Romano, 16

P

Peaches
Brandied Peaches & Cream, 224
Chicken with Peach-Champagne Sauce, 84
Peach Tapioca, 242
Peachy Smothered Pork Chops, 140
Peach Tapioca, 242
Peachy Smothered Pork Chops, 140
Peanutty Chocolate Fudge, 238
Pecan Cheese Ball, 20

Index

Pineapple
Ambrosia, 122
Chunky Hawaiian Spread, 118
Hawaiian Ribs, 130
Hawaiian-Style Burgers, 136
Marinated Flank Steak with Pineapple, 146
Mixed Grill Kabobs, 148
Pineapple-Ginger Shrimp Cocktail, 116
Pineapple Upside-Down Cake, 180
Spam™ Hawaiian Pizza, 116
Tropical Luau Cupcakes, 134
Tropical Pork Chops, 129
Wild Hawaiian Cocktail Meatballs, 17
Pineapple-Ginger Shrimp Cocktail, 116
Pineapple Upside-Down Cake, 180
Pink Peppermint Meringues, 202
Pork Schnitzel, 36
Pork (*see also* **Ham & Canned Meat; Sausage**), **32–59**
Grilled Sherry Pork Chops, 157
Hawaiian Ribs, 130
Herb Orange Pork Chops, 160
Hungarian Goulash Casserole, 110
Javanese Pork Saté, 149
Mixed Grill Kabobs, 148
Peachy Smothered Pork Chops, 140
Tropical Pork Chops, 129
Pretty-in-Pink Peppermint Cupcakes, 172
Puff Pastry
Beef Wellington, 50
Chicken Wellington, 86
Spam® à la King, 52
Pumpkin Pecan Rum Cake, 174

Q
Quick and Easy Jumbles, 213

R
Raspberry: Raspberry Topping, 241
Rice
Chicken Bourguignonne, 71
Chicken Cordon Bleu, 78
Chicken Divan Casserole, 100
Rice Pudding, 236
Salmon Casserole, 90
Seafood Newburg Casserole, 108
Spanish Rice & Chicken Skillet, 76
Wild Hawaiian Cocktail Meatballs, 17
Rice Pudding, 236
Roast Pork Chops with Apple and Cabbage, 40
Rocky Road Brownies, 220
Rum Butter Glaze, 174

S
Salmon
Salmon Casserole, 90
Smoked Salmon Appetizers, 26
Salmon Casserole, 90
Sausage
Country Sausage Macaroni and Cheese, 104
Mixed Grill Kabobs, 148
Scalloped Apples & Onions, 98
Scalloped Garlic Potatoes, 96
Scallops
Brandy-Soaked Scallops, 14
Seafood Newburg Casserole, 108
Seafood Newburg Casserole, 108
Seafood (*see also individual varieties*):
California Seafood Dip, 22
Sensational Spinach Dip, 22
Shrimp
Pineapple-Ginger Shrimp Cocktail, 116
Seafood Newburg Casserole, 108
Shrimp Toasts, 24

Index

Shrimp (*continued*)
South Seas Shrimp & Mango, 126
Surf & Turf Kabobs, 162
Sirloin Steak Monte Carlo, 41
Smoked Salmon Appetizers, 26
Soup, Canned
Beef Stroganoff Casserole, 102
Chicken, Asparagus & Mushroom Bake, 112
Chicken Tetrazzini, 106
Classic Turkey Pot Pie, 92
Crunchy Veg•All® Tuna Casserole, 92
Down-Home Pork and Beans, 38
Hearty Shepherd's Pie, 97
Homestyle Chicken Pot Pie, 70
Hungarian Goulash Casserole, 110
Manhattan Turkey à la King, 62
Salmon Casserole, 90
Seafood Newburg Casserole, 108
Souperior Meat Loaf, 54
Southern Buttermilk Fried Chicken, 64
South Seas Shrimp & Mango, 126
Spam® à la King, 52
Spam™ Cornbread Pie, 94
Spam™ Hawaiian Pizza, 116
Spanish Rice & Chicken Skillet, 76
Spiced Grilled Bananas, 124
Spicy Spam™ Party Dip, 16
Spinach: Sensational Spinach Dip, 22
Steak Hash, 38
Strawberry
Creamy Coconut-Lime Fruit Salad, 118
Strawberry Stripe Refrigerator Cake, 192
Surf & Turf Kabobs, 162
Swedish Meatballs, 48
Sweetheart Chocolate Mousse, 232
Sweet Potatoes: Mashed Sweet Potatoes, 150

T
Tamale Pie, 105
Tidal Wave Cocoa Almond Mousse, 128
Toll House® Famous Fudge, 238
Tomatoes, Fresh
Blue Crab Stuffed Tomatoes, 18
Country Sausage Macaroni and Cheese, 104
Tropical Luau Cupcakes, 134
Tropical Pork Chops, 129
Tuna
Crunchy Veg•All® Tuna Casserole, 92
Tuna Mushroom Pâté with Orange Liqueur, 28
Turkey
Classic Turkey Pot Pie, 92
Manhattan Turkey à la King, 62

V
Veal
Double Cheese Veal Cutlets, 34
Veal Scallopini, 56
Veg•All® Beef & Cheddar Bake, 96
Vegetables, Mixed
Classic Turkey Pot Pie, 92
Crunchy Veg•All® Tuna Casserole, 92
Hearty Shepherd's Pie, 97
Homestyle Chicken Pot Pie, 70
Veg•All® Beef & Cheddar Bake, 96
Venetian Canapés, 30

W
Wild Hawaiian Cocktail Meatballs, 17

Z
Zesty Liver Pâté, 26

Metric Conversion Chart

VOLUME MEASUREMENTS (dry)

$^1/_8$ teaspoon = 0.5 mL
$^1/_4$ teaspoon = 1 mL
$^1/_2$ teaspoon = 2 mL
$^3/_4$ teaspoon = 4 mL
1 teaspoon = 5 mL
1 tablespoon = 15 mL
2 tablespoons = 30 mL
$^1/_4$ cup = 60 mL
$^1/_3$ cup = 75 mL
$^1/_2$ cup = 125 mL
$^2/_3$ cup = 150 mL
$^3/_4$ cup = 175 mL
1 cup = 250 mL
2 cups = 1 pint = 500 mL
3 cups = 750 mL
4 cups = 1 quart = 1 L

VOLUME MEASUREMENTS (fluid)

1 fluid ounce (2 tablespoons) = 30 mL
4 fluid ounces ($^1/_2$ cup) = 125 mL
8 fluid ounces (1 cup) = 250 mL
12 fluid ounces (1$^1/_2$ cups) = 375 mL
16 fluid ounces (2 cups) = 500 mL

WEIGHTS (mass)

$^1/_2$ ounce = 15 g
1 ounce = 30 g
3 ounces = 90 g
4 ounces = 120 g
8 ounces = 225 g
10 ounces = 285 g
12 ounces = 360 g
16 ounces = 1 pound = 450 g

DIMENSIONS

$^1/_{16}$ inch = 2 mm
$^1/_8$ inch = 3 mm
$^1/_4$ inch = 6 mm
$^1/_2$ inch = 1.5 cm
$^3/_4$ inch = 2 cm
1 inch = 2.5 cm

OVEN TEMPERATURES

250°F = 120°C
275°F = 140°C
300°F = 150°C
325°F = 160°C
350°F = 180°C
375°F = 190°C
400°F = 200°C
425°F = 220°C
450°F = 230°C

BAKING PAN SIZES

Utensil	Size in Inches/Quarts	Metric Volume	Size in Centimeters
Baking or Cake Pan (square or rectangular)	8×8×2	2 L	20×20×5
	9×9×2	2.5 L	23×23×5
	12×8×2	3 L	30×20×5
	13×9×2	3.5 L	33×23×5
Loaf Pan	8×4×3	1.5 L	20×10×7
	9×5×3	2 L	23×13×7
Round Layer Cake Pan	8×1½	1.2 L	20×4
	9×1½	1.5 L	23×4
Pie Plate	8×1¼	750 mL	20×3
	9×1¼	1 L	23×3
Baking Dish or Casserole	1 quart	1 L	—
	1½ quart	1.5 L	—
	2 quart	2 L	—